PRAISE FOR

GOD'S PURPOSE FOR YOUR LIFE

I have received so much edification from all of Barbara Wentroble's books; however, in writing *God's Purpose for Your Life* I believe she has reached a new level. I'll admit that I "cheated" and read the testimonies at the end of each chapter first and got so excited I couldn't wait to dive into the rest of the book! I did find it difficult to read at times . . . only because of my tears as I wept. It seemed as if Barbara had written this book just for me.

You will also be impacted as Barbara, in her easy-to-understand way of communicating, takes you from being the "called" to being the "chosen" to being the "faithful." This book will definitely help many on their journey to fulfilling their destiny in Christ.

DOUG FORTUNE
TRUMPET CALL MINISTRY
MCPHERSON, KANSAS

No believer in Christ escapes His call—it is the genesis of all our experience and ministry. God calls and our response releases our destiny. Barbara Wentroble weaves inspiring personal testimonies with biblical insights that tell us how to overcome the obstacles that inevitably follow our initial call to minister for God in every sphere of life. This motivational and practical book will be a good tool to work maturity into the Body of Christ.

JIM HODGES, APOSTOLIC TEAM LEADER
FEDERATION OF MINISTERS AND CHURCHES, INC.
DALLAS, TEXAS

If you do not know what God has intended for your life, you will not achieve His destiny for you. *God's Purpose for Your Life* will give you the revelation and knowledge to take aim and focus on His perfect plan. I strongly encourage you to read this excellent book from this apostolic prophetess Barbara Wentroble.

APOSTLE JOHN P. KELLY
PRESIDENT OF LEAD (LEADERSHIP EDUCATION FOR APOSTOLIC DEVELOPMENT)
AMBASSADOR APOSTLE OF INTERNATIONAL COALITION OF APOSTLES

Many are called but few are chosen! God's call to each of our lives moves through a process of covenant alignment and our becoming faithful to the Creator of our life and purpose. Barbara Wentroble captures with simplicity this complex process. The call of God to anyone includes many tests of faith. Many times we give up the familiar, deny ourselves and sacrifice in ways that go against our understanding. If we choose to follow and become faithful, we are grafted into God's covenant blessing. *God's Purpose for Your Life* is important for anyone to read, so they can understand where they are in God's ultimate plan in their life. This book is one of the few books that transcends the generations. Anyone—young or old— at any stage of life should read this book.

DR. CHUCK D. PIERCE
VICE PRESIDENT, GLOBAL HARVEST MINISTRIES
GLORY OF ZION MINISTRIES

It is obvious that as you read Barbara's book *God's Purpose for Your Life*, you will see that she has experienced the battles necessary for the anointing. This book is filled with personal stories, both hers and those of other national leaders. I love it! What is so wonderful about Barbara Wentroble is that she is real and transparent. I recommend you get her book today!

ALICE SMITH
EXECUTIVE DIRECTOR
U.S. PRAYER CENTER, HOUSTON, TEXAS

This book is simply terrific and should be required reading for everyone who has a call from God. Today many people are desperately searching for resources that will help them move forward in their call. I have looked for such a book to which I can refer people. This book is it—a primer for all who have received a call from God. It sets forth how to confirm the call, proceed through the preparation process and arrive at the destination called fulfillment. Furthermore, anyone who becomes grounded in God's Word and follows what Barbara sets forth will not only start well but will also finish well. Barbara herself is a great example of this. Those who follow the path she sets forth will be a demonstration of the mightiness of God manifested through a single human being.

BARBARA J. YODER
SENIOR PASTOR AND GREAT LAKES/MIDWEST REGIONAL STRATEGIC PRAYER
NETWORK COORDINATOR (USSPN)

GOD'S PURPOSE *for* YOUR LIFE

Barbara Wentroble

Regal

From Gospel Light
Ventura, California, U.S.A.

Published by Regal Books
From Gospel Light
Ventura, California, U.S.A.
Printed in the U.S.A.

Regal Books is a ministry of Gospel Light, an evangelical Christian publisher dedicated to serving the local church. We believe God's vision for Gospel Light is to provide church leaders with biblical, user-friendly materials that will help them evangelize, disciple and minister to children, youth and families.

It is our prayer that this Regal book will help you discover biblical truth for your own life and help you meet the needs of others. May God richly bless you.

For a free catalog of resources from Regal Books/Gospel Light, please call your Christian supplier or contact us at 1-800-4-GOSPEL *or* www.regalbooks.com.

Cover and Interior Design by Robert Williams
Edited by Kathi Macias and Rose Decaen

LIBRARY OF CONGRESS CATALOGING-IN-PUBLICATION DATA
Wentroble, Barbara, 1943-
   God's purpose for your life / Barbara Wentroble.
      p.   cm.
Includes bibliographical references.
   ISBN 0-8307-2929-1 (trade paper)
   1.   Vocation—Biblical teaching.   I. Title.
   BS680.V6 W46 2002
   248.4—dc21   2001007605

1 2 3 4 5 6 7 8 9 10 11 12 13 14 15 / 09 08 07 06 05 04 03 02

Rights for publishing this book in other languages are contracted by Gospel Light Worldwide, the international nonprofit ministry of Gospel Light. Gospel Light Worldwide also provides publishing and technical assistance to international publishers dedicated to producing Sunday School and Vacation Bible School curricula and books in the languages of the world. For additional information, visit www.gospellightworldwide.org; write to Gospel Light Worldwide, P.O. Box 3875, Ventura, CA 93006; or send an e-mail to info@gospellightworldwide.org.

DEDICATION

To my precious granddaughters,
Lindsey and Kailee.
May you go farther in the Lord than
I and my generation
or
your parents and their generation.
May you faithfully declare to your generation
the purpose of God.
You have been brought into the Kingdom
for such a time as this!

CONTENTS

Foreword. 11

Introduction. 13
Called, Chosen and Faithful

SECTION I: THE CALLED

Chapter 1 16
Recognizing God's Call on Your Life

Chapter 2 27
Responding to the Call

Chapter 3 38
Growing in the Call

Chapter 4 52
A Firm Foundation for the Call

Chapter 5 63
Called to Different Arenas of Life

SECTION II: THE CHOSEN

Chapter 6 76
Why Is All This Happening?

Chapter 7 88
The Fourth Man in the Furnace

Chapter 8 100
Receiving a New Identity

Chapter 9 113
Relationships for Destiny

Chapter 10 124
Overcoming Jezebel and Controlling Spirits

SECTION III: THE FAITHFUL

Chapter 11 138
Breaking out of the Old Place

Chapter 12 149
Transition Challenges

Chapter 13 160
New Level, New Devil

Chapter 14 174
Mentoring the Next Generation

Chapter 15 184
Eagles of God

FOREWORD

Some Christian books, in all honesty, answer questions no one seems to be asking, but not this one. Of all of the questions we can ask ourselves, one of the most important and exciting is, What is God's purpose for my life? Inside each of us, if we truly long to serve God, is a hunger to know why we are here on planet Earth. Each of us has surely wondered, *What is the call of God on my life?* Another way to put this is, What was God up to when He created me?

God's response, of course, varies from believer to believer. Sometimes His expectations are clear. At other times they may seem cloudy. However, with solid spiritual moorings and mentoring, each Christian *can* discover God's purpose for his or her life—and Barbara Wentroble has written this book to show you how you can discover yours.

Barbara and I frequently speak at the same conferences, and we serve together on the boards of various ministries. Through the years, I have come to greatly esteem her deep insights and knack for cutting to the key issues. In *God's Purpose for Your Life*, Barbara applies these abilities as she reveals essential strategies to finding and fulfilling your purpose. She illustrates how it is vital to first receive, understand and grow in the specific call of God. She then moves you through the stages of development in your purpose, including the tough times of spiritual refinement via a "spiritual furnace" and how to come out transformed, with a new identity, in shape to fully move forward. Finally, she mentors you in how to step up to the next level, in faith.

Barbara does not simply tell us to find our purpose; rather, she guides the reader along each step. Then she paints the picture of how it works by including true stories of believers who have found their calls and flourished in their purposes. How inspiring to read these real stories of God in action in the lives of those who chose to follow His call! I encourage each of you to be a student and to find your purpose.

Do you want to be who God created you to be? Of course you do! So I invite you to read this book. My dear friend Barbara Wentroble has done her research and has lived out the lesson. Not only does she delve into the biblical guidelines on this important question, but she also demonstrates how it has worked in her own life and how it can work in your life. Barbara reveals how God's purpose is not some daunting mystery that may someday fall upon us. She demystifies "the call," making it something that, once you know it, can and will totally change how you serve the Lord. After you read *God's Purpose for Your Life,* the question will not be, Does God have a purpose for my life? It will be, When can I start moving in that purpose?

Dutch Sheets
Colorado Springs, Colorado

CALLED, CHOSEN AND FAITHFUL

An emerging generation of people is coming forth to advance the kingdom of God. As they mature in their callings, they will fulfill their destinies in the Lord. The Bible mentions this company of people as they progress through three stages of development. Those three stages in life are called, chosen and faithful.

> These will wage war against the Lamb, and the Lamb will overcome them, because He is Lord of lords and King of kings, and those who are with Him are the called and chosen and faithful (Rev. 17:14).

In *God's Purpose for Your Life*, I discuss both the good and the difficult times during a person's development process for his or her destiny.

Many people do not arrive at the potential God has for them because they do not understand the process. After getting excited over an experience with God, they drop out along the way. These encounters with God are designed to propel us onto a path of victory and achievement.

Frequently I am asked by people to help mentor them as they walk with the Lord. Many sense a call of God on their lives but are unable to find someone who can help them come into the fullness of the call. Few books about spiritual mentoring are available on the market to help these individuals. *God's Purpose for Your Life* will help fill this void.

At the end of each chapter I have included a real-life story. Recognized authors and other individuals have written personal testimonies about a time in their lives when they experienced the subject matter of each chapter. You will find each story a source of strength as you walk a similar path.

May the Lord bless you as you pursue the call He has on your life. May He strengthen you as you press forward through the difficult places. May you arrive at your destiny with an anointing to help change individuals, cities and nations. May you hear the voice of the Lord as He commends you for being faithful to your call.

> Well done, you upright—honorable, admirable—and faithful servant! You have been faithful and trustworthy over a little; I will put you in charge of much. Enter into and share the joy— the delight, the blessedness—which your master enjoys (Matt. 25:21, *AMP*).

THE CALLED

For many are called, but few are chosen.

MATTHEW 22:14

CHAPTER 1

RECOGNIZING GOD'S CALL ON YOUR LIFE

I sat listening intently as the speaker talked about the pruning process God has for our lives. All of this was so new to me. Although I had been a Christian since age 12, I was not accustomed to this type of meeting. Only a couple weeks earlier I had come into the fullness of the Holy Spirit. After the message, the speaker gave "words from the Lord." I had never heard this done before. How could anyone be sure the words were really from God? I didn't know the Lord spoke to people like that today.

"There is someone here today, and when you were a little girl," the speaker said, "you told the Lord, 'I'll be a missionary for You.' The Lord wants you to know you will be a missionary for Him, just not in the way you thought." The words seemed to go right into my heart. Suddenly, I saw a picture of the Sunday School room where I had attended church when I was nine years old. I could even see the small window at the top of one of the walls. While watching this scene play out in my memory, I heard myself say, "Lord, I'll be a missionary for You."

Now, at age 31, I was a wife and a mother of three small children. How could I have forgotten my conversation with the Lord? How could I have forgotten my commitment to His call? Yet somehow, in the busyness of life, I had not remembered. Even so, God remembered.

As I pondered the memory, questions flooded my mind.

• *What did the Lord mean when He said I would be a missionary but not in the way I thought?*

- *What other kinds of missionaries are there?*
- *How could I keep my commitment to the Lord and still be a wife and mother?*
- *Did the Lord expect me to pick up my family and move to Africa? (That was my impression of a "real" missionary.)*
- *What would happen if my husband did not want to go to Africa?*

THE BEGINNING OF A PROCESS

For the first time in many years, I recognized that the Lord was calling me. Later, He would reinforce that call in a variety of ways. But at that time, I realized the sovereign God of the universe still speaks to people today and calls them for His purposes. Although the Lord had affirmed His call, it was only the beginning of a process. The journey had just started. Years would be spent dreaming, praying, studying, trying, stumbling, getting up and going again. Some days would be mountaintop experiences. Other days would look more like valleys. None of that changed the mind of the Lord, however, nor His call on my life. I would later learn that I was created to fulfill the destiny He had for me. You have been created for God's purposes, as well. Every believer has a call from the Lord. The specific calls are different and come in different ways, but God calls each of us to fulfill a unique destiny.

> The entire New Testament exhorts that no matter what our lineage, talents, gender, social or marital status, once we have accepted Christ as our personal Savior, there is a calling to which each of us must personally respond. With that calling comes an enabling anointing to carry out the call.[1]

Throughout the Bible, we find stories of many people called by God. He did not use the same method to call each of them. God speaks in numerous ways, and many times God calls, but individuals often do not recognize His voice.

In the Bible the Lord called young Samuel. Although God was speaking, Samuel did not immediately recognize God's voice (see 1 Sam. 3:1-21).

God speaks regularly, but our spiritual ears have not learned how to recognize His voice.

I grew up in a church that taught me God does not speak to people today. Therefore, I did not expect Him to speak to me. How amazed I was when the "word of the Lord" went into my heart at the meeting that day. Somehow, I knew at that moment that God was speaking. No matter what I had been taught, my experience with the Lord could not be denied.

THE DIFFERENT WAYS GOD SPEAKS

The Lord had spoken to me through two of the manifestation gifts of the Holy Spirit, known as the "word of knowledge" and "prophecy." All nine of these manifestation gifts are listed in 1 Corinthians 12:7-10. These supernatural gifts are available to the believer for empowerment for service to the Lord. The gifts are not *natural* but *supernatural*. The gift called the word of knowledge is supernatural knowledge related to a fact. The fact can be something that existed in the past or something that exists now. That I had made a commitment to the Lord was a fact that existed in the past. The speaker did not know *everything* about me. She only received a small amount of knowledge from the Lord concerning me—a "word." The gift known as prophecy means speaking the mind of God by the inspiration of the Holy Spirit and not from one's own thoughts. Both gifts were in operation through the speaker that day.

Evidently, in the New Testament, the call on Timothy's life came in a similar way.

> This command I entrust to you, Timothy, my son, in accordance with the prophecies previously made concerning you, that by them you may fight the good fight (1 Tim. 1:18).

Paul was exhorting young Timothy to remember the call on his life that had been spoken through the supernatural gift of prophecy. He was to use the word from the Lord as a weapon of warfare to press through the hindrances to his call.

Another way God calls people is through dreams and visions. Dutch Sheets shares in his book *Intercessory Prayer* how the Lord revealed to him the Lord's call for youth. Dutch was called to be a major participant in the coming revival. There was a time when he and his wife, Ceci, attended the National Day of Prayer meeting in Washington, D.C., with a group of young people. Several months prior, Dutch had seen a vision of a stadium filled with young people who would be instruments of the Lord to help bring revival to our nation. While attending the prayer conference, the Lord spoke several other confirmations to Dutch concerning the importance of youth as a vital ingredient of revival. During this time, he was scheduled to be a participant in the reading of the Bible while facing the Capitol. Each participant would read for 15 minutes. The specific Bible passages to be read were assigned by someone else. Dutch asked the Lord to confirm to him that what he had seen in the vision was from God. He wanted to be sure the vision of revival among youth was a true call from the Lord.

> Due to the nature of the Lord's dealings with me at that time, I told him, "Lord, there is only one way I could know of a certainty that You are confirming these things to me through my Bible reading. When I arrive, they must tell me that I can either read the book of Habakkuk or Haggai." This was not a fleece, nor was I testing God. It was because of the things I had already sensed Him saying to me through these two books.[2]

As the time approached for Dutch to read from the Bible, a lady walked up and spoke to him. "You are on in 15 minutes, after this person. You have your choice. You can either read the book of Haggai or the book of Habakkuk." Dutch had his confirmation that the vision he had seen was from the Lord!

Visions and dreams are supernatural ways God speaks to people. Dreams occur when we are asleep. Visions are similar to dreams, but visions occur when a person is awake. Joseph received his call through a dream when he was a teenager.

> He said to them, "Please listen to this dream which I have had; for behold, we were binding sheaves in the field, and lo, my sheaf rose up and also stood erect; and behold, your sheaves gathered around and bowed down to my sheaf" (Gen. 37:6-7).

In the dream Joseph knew God was calling him to a position in life where his own family would honor him. As one of the younger children in the family, Joseph was not in line for this privilege. Nevertheless, God had called Joseph for a specific destiny that would affect not only his family but also nations.

The apostle Paul received the call to Macedonia through a vision.

A vision appeared to Paul in the night: a certain man of Macedonia was standing and appealing to him, and saying, "Come over to Macedonia and help us." And when he had seen the vision, immediately we sought to go into Macedonia, concluding that God had called us to preach the gospel to them (Acts 16:9-10).

God's communication of His call is found as a normal way of life throughout the Bible. Dr. C. Peter Wagner mentions this in his book *The Acts of the Holy Spirit.*

Those who have a first-century pre-Enlightenment worldview such as Paul had, would not consider it unusual for supernatural beings—angels of darkness as well as angels of light—to communicate with human beings through visions and dreams. For example, Paul's conversion experience on the road to Damascus also included a vision in which he actually saw Jesus. . . . Visions were such an assumed part of common life that there is no telling how many other visions Paul might have had between his conversion some 16 years previously and now.[3]

God also calls people by way of the Scriptures. Frequently, He chooses to use this powerful means to speak or call to His people. The Bible must be our foundation for life. As we read, study and meditate on God's Word, we know the will of the Lord.

In the Old Testament the High Priest had two objects he would use when needing the decision of the Lord. They were called the Urim and the Thummim, and they were placed in the breastplate of the priest's garments. The meaning of the names of these objects is "lights" and "perfection," respectively. Therefore, we need "Spirit" and "word" to know the will of the Lord. As we are reading and studying the Bible, God will cause His Spirit to illuminate the Scriptures so that we can know His will.

But as we seek guidance from Scripture, we must be careful to observe basic rules of interpretation. We must see what the text says in light of the context. If there is a question, we may need to check the translation with the original text. Then we must look to see if it falls into a cultural setting or if it is a basic principle of scripture for all times.

Above all, to hear God speak to us from scriptures, we must allow the Holy Spirit to illumine God's Word. Jesus said, "When He, the Spirit of truth, comes, He will guide you into all the truth" (John 16:13). The Holy Spirit takes one portion of the scriptures, brings it to life for us, and applies it to the present circumstances.[4]

DISCERNMENT: LEARNING TO HEAR FROM GOD

Most times when God calls someone, He places an inner knowing on the inside of the person. The individual has a deep understanding in his or her spirit that the Lord has called him or her for a special purpose. Sometimes the person senses the voice of the Lord speaking to him or her. At other times there is merely an assurance that the Lord has called. Cindy Jacobs described this way of God's calling in her book *The Voice of God*.

As years passed, the Lord began to make it clear to me in various ways that he was calling me to "something"—such as the time when I was at junior church camp in Prescott, Arizona, at nine years of age. One day our counselor encouraged each of us to find a quiet place to "talk with God." I remember crawling up on a huge rock outside the chapel. As I was lying back on that rough granite rock, surrounded by the visible manifestations of God's artistry of blue sky and towering trees, I began to pray, "Lord, what do you want from my life?" At first, all I heard was the sound of the wind and trees harmonizing with the birds in the woods. Then I quietly heard another sound—it was the Voice of God saying, "Cindy, I have something I want for you to do for Me." At the sound of His Voice spoken so sweetly in my soul, I responded with my heart beating staccato along with the wind and trees, "Here am I, Lord, send me." I can still hear the words as strongly as the day He spoke them to me.[5]

In the Bible, a young child by the name of Samuel received a calling by hearing the voice of the Lord. He did not recognize God's voice the first time God called him. It is common for people to not recognize the voice of the Lord, because they have not developed a sensitivity to hear with their spiritual ears.

Eli the priest discerned the Lord was trying to speak to Samuel. After Eli instructed Samuel to go back and listen for the Lord's voice, Samuel was able to hear more clearly. He then heard the Lord calling his name and received a word concerning the future of Eli's family.

> Then the LORD came and stood and called as at other times, "Samuel! Samuel!" And Samuel said, "Speak, for Thy servant is listening" (1 Sam. 3:10).

God has such a powerful voice that He even calls to the elements and to creatures. Such created things are able to hear the Lord and respond to His calling.

> When He utters His voice, there is a tumult of waters in the heavens, and He causes the clouds to ascend from the end of the earth; He makes lightning for the rain, and brings forth the wind from His storehouses (Jer. 51:16).

> Then I will make up to you for the years that the swarming locust has eaten, the creeping locust, the stripping locust, and

the gnawing locust, My great army which I sent among you (Joel 2:25).

He said to them, "Why are you timid, you men of little faith?" Then He arose, and rebuked the winds and the sea; and it became perfectly calm. And the men marveled, saying, "What kind of a man is this, that even the winds and the sea obey Him?" (Matt. 8:26-27).

A SPECIAL PLACE AND A SPECIFIC CALL

God is a loving father who desires to communicate with His children. He knows each one of us so intimately that the Bible says He even numbers the hair on each head (see Matt. 10:30). A special place and a specific call are issued to each of God's children. Frank Damazio, in his book *The Making of a Leader*, wrote that all believers are called to a specific function.

> The call of God has two sides that make a perfectly balanced whole. The necessity of a divine call cannot be stressed enough, when we have many presuming upon the offices of the governmental ministries described in Ephesians 4:11. Unfortunately, the Church herself has helped create some of the confusion. She has over-emphasized the five gifted ministries, and has not taught enough about every-member ministry. Some people believed that governmental ministries were the only ones available. They falsely assumed that if they wanted to serve God and His Church, they had to aspire to one of the governmental ministries. . . . Though there are different callings in the Body, all of the callings are important and necessary. The difference lies in function, not in importance.[6]

Regardless of the method God uses to call a person, there must be an inner witness of God's divine call. Powerful prophets can prophesy the call on a person's life. Friends and family can speak volumes of encouragement. Hands can be laid on the individual. Ordination and legal documents can be conferred. Yet the most crucial requirement of the call is that the individual has an inner witness. A person may not understand the details of the call. It may be years before the manifestation of the call emerges. Still, that person must experience an inner witness in the spirit that God has issued a call.

The inner assurance of the divine call from God will be the strength needed in times of difficulty. I have a friend who had a favorite saying: "Be sure of the call when your back is up against the wall." How often I have remembered that exhortation when I have been in hard places!

Once you are assured of God's call on your life, He will send others to encourage you. Through the years, when I did not understand God's call, He sent prophets to prophesy the call to me. Scriptures seemed to jump off the pages of the Bible to encourage me. Preachers would speak right to my heart and my situation. God opened doors to develop the call. For many years I did not understand how all these pieces of the puzzle would fit together. As I look back now, I can see the Lord's hand directing me in my call. He will do the same for you. God wants you to know He has called you.

As a young child sitting in the Sunday School classroom, I thought I was letting the Lord know what I wanted to do for Him. How little I knew that it was the Lord putting His desire in my heart, so I could respond to His call when it came!

Delight yourself in the LORD; And He will give you the desires of your heart (Ps. 37:4).

Some people develop a false humility by denying they want a call from the Lord. Do the most humble thing you can do: Delight yourself in the Lord. Then allow Him to put a deep desire in your heart for His call. He will also delight in your wanting to fulfill His destiny for your life. Desires will come into your heart from the Spirit of the Lord. The most exciting thing you will ever do is to hear the call of God for your life. Then you can allow Him to orchestrate your steps into your divine destiny!

THE REAL STORY
RECOGNIZING GOD'S CALL ON MY LIFE

Testimony by Dr. Chuck D. Pierce
Executive Vice President of Global Harvest, Colorado Springs
Founding President of Glory of Zion Ministries, Denton, Texas

The call of God is a covenant call. When I was 18 years old, I had strayed from His ultimate will. In His sovereignty and love, He searched me out and turned me toward Himself. I had experienced a physical struggle and was hospitalized. God placed a Pentecostal pastor in the room. He shared God's love and Spirit. After this, I found myself in the presence of almighty God for three days.

I immediately had the pursuit of God in my heart. I went to the Baptist Student Union State Convention in Texas. While I was in the balcony on Missions Night, I heard the Spirit of God speak, "I have called you for the healing of the nations." I was clueless to what this meant; but I went forward, surrendered and filled out a card that said I would serve in missions. Even though I had no understanding about this call, the Lord began to supernaturally orchestrate my life. For example, I noticed at the altar a beautiful red-haired lady, Pam, who later became my wife.

The call of God to anyone is a call that includes many tests of faith. Many times we give up the familiar, deny ourselves and sacrifice in ways that go against our understanding. However, when we choose to follow, we are grafted into God's Covenant blessing that He spoke to Abraham. From that call, He can make you a great nation, bless you, make your name great, cause you to be a blessing, prosper and multiply you and cause many around you to be blessed (see Gen. 12:2-3).

As I now travel throughout the world, I fully understand the ultimate purpose that God had for me when He extended His grace to unlock my destiny. If He's calling you today, heed His voice and follow after Him.

DISCUSSION QUESTIONS

1. Have you received a call from God?
2. If yes, describe the way God called you.
3. Why do we need the supernatural gifts of the Holy Spirit listed in 1 Corinthians 12?
4. What is the difference between a dream and a vision?
5. Describe a couple of people in the Bible who received a call from God. What methods did the Lord use to call them?
6. Why does a person need an "inner knowing" concerning God's call on his life?
7. What happens when an individual delights himself in the Lord? Are you delighting in the Lord today? Expect an encounter with the Lord!

Notes

1. Glenda Malmin, *Woman, You Are Called and Anointed* (Portland, OR: City Bible Publishers, 1998), p. 16.
2. Dutch Sheets, *Intercessory Prayer* (Ventura, CA: Regal Books, 1996), pp. 228-29.
3. C. Peter Wagner, *The Acts of the Holy Spirit* (Ventura, CA: Regal Books, 2000), p. 388.
4. Herman Riffel, *Learning to Hear God's Voice* (Old Tappan, NJ: Chosen Books, 1986), pp. 51-52.
5. Cindy Jacobs, *The Voice of God* (Ventura, CA: Regal Books, 1995), pp. 21-22.
6. Frank Damazio, *The Making of a Leader* (Portland, OR: City Bible Publishing, 1988), p. 40.

CHAPTER 2

RESPONDING TO THE CALL

We had only lived in the neighborhood for a couple of weeks. I had just met my new neighbor, who seemed extremely frustrated with her five-year-old son. "Danny! Danny, stop climbing on the fence!" she yelled repeatedly. "You'll fall!"

Getting no response from her little one, she turned and looked at me, completely baffled. "I don't know whether it's a discipline problem or a hearing problem," she lamented. I was sure I had the answer for her. It was apparent that the child was healthy and quite capable of hearing—he simply failed to respond correctly to what he was hearing.

RESPONDING IN OBEDIENCE—
OR DISOBEDIENCE

How often do we do the same thing with the Lord? Even after we understand that God has called us, we do one of two things: We respond obediently or disobediently. These are the only options. Fulfilled destiny hinges on our response. My response to the Lord as a young child in that Sunday School room was one of obedience—at the moment. However, I lacked the understanding of how to embrace the call by focusing upon it, so the Lord could direct my steps. As a result, I experienced many unfruitful years in the pursuit of my call.

One heart response of obedience is to acknowledge God's call by faith. It is not necessary to know the fullness of the call or how God will use you at this point. Understanding and vision will come as you move forward. Noah was a man of faith. When the Lord spoke to him about preparing an ark for a coming flood, he had little understanding of his call. Up until that time, there had never been rain. The Lord watered the Earth by a mist that came up from the ground. Noah did not have someone as a model who previously had built an ark. He merely responded to the Lord in faith and allowed the Lord to instruct him along the way.

> Without faith it is impossible to please Him, for he who comes to God must believe that He is, and that He is a rewarder of those who seek Him. By faith Noah, being warned by God about things not yet seen, in reverence prepared an ark for the salvation of his household, by which he condemned the world, and became an heir of the righteousness which is according to faith (Heb. 11:6-7).

Another positive response to the Lord's call is one of humility. Often we have an idea of what God's plan for our future may be. Sometimes we may see ourselves standing before thousands of people or as the president of some very large corporation. God may do these things in our lives; He may not. A response of humility opens the door for the Lord's promotion to wherever He wants to use us.

> Humble yourselves in the presence of the Lord, and He will exalt you (Jas. 4:10).

A spirit of humility is not developed through a one-time event. Rather, humility is a way of life, and great leaders understand the cost that must be paid for greatness.

Sacrifice is often linked with humility. A life of humility may involve doing jobs for which you are overqualified. Loss of finances may be required. Forgiving those who have wronged you is vital. Pride and self-importance cannot operate in a person who walks in humility. A willingness to do whatever is necessary to see others advance and seek their goals and the goals of the Kingdom above our own interests is essential.

John C. Maxwell is a well-known contemporary writer on leadership principles. He maintains that cost is involved in becoming a successful leader. Maxwell believes most people accept the fact that sacrifice is involved in the initial stages of their life purpose, but he also contends that sacrifice is more than an initial requirement. Sacrifice is a constant in leadership—it is the price involved when coming into prominence.

> Leaders who want to rise have to do more than take an occasional cut in pay. They have to give up their rights. As my friend Gerald Brooks says, "When you become a leader, you lose the right to think about yourself." For every person, the nature of the sacrifice may be different. For example, Iacocca's greatest sacrifices came late in his career. In the case of someone like South African president F. W. deKlerk, who worked to dismantle apartheid in his country, the cost was his career itself. The circumstances may change from person to person, but the principle doesn't. Leadership means sacrifice.[1]

I love the way Doug Fortune describes humility.

> True humility is not about US; it is about Christ IN US. My most humble effort still has the stench of pride, because it is MY effort. You see, Christ has already provided a humility for us to walk in . . . it is called being "conformable unto HIS Death." Jesus said, "I can of mine OWN SELF do nothing . . ." (John 5:30), yet people were healed, delivered, even raised from the dead in His ministry. Did this cause Him to be lifted up in pride? . . . No, because He understood that it was the work of His Father.
>
> If I understand that I am DEAD in Christ and it is His LIFE being lived in me and through me, THEN He is able to do abundantly above anything I could ask or think! Then He is not limited in what He can do through me.[2]

Humility and meekness often are associated (see Eph. 4:2; Col. 3:12). *Strong's Concordance* defines "humility" as "condescension, gentleness, meekness."[3] A spirit of humility and meekness leads a person into success in life.

> The reward of humility and the fear of the LORD are riches, honor and life (Prov. 22:4).

Meekness is not weakness! It is strength under the control of the Holy Spirit. In the Greek language the word for "meekness" is *prautes*. *Vine's Expository Dictionary of New Testament Words* defines the strength associated with a spirit of meekness.

> The meaning of *prautes* is not readily expressed in English, for the terms meekness, mildness, commonly used, suggest weakness and pusillanimity to a greater or less extent, whereas *prautes* does nothing of the kind. . . . It must be clearly understood, therefore, that the meekness manifested by the Lord and commended to the believer is the fruit of power. The common assumption is that when a man is meek it is because he cannot help himself; but the Lord was "meek" because he had the infinite resources of God at His command. Described negatively, meekness is the opposite to self-assertiveness and self-interest; it is equanimity of spirit that is neither elated nor cast down, simply because it is not occupied with self at all.[4]

Meekness can be portrayed as a wild horse that is now tamed and under the control of the bit and bridle. The horse has not lost his strength. He has merely allowed the strength to be brought under the control of the master. As we allow the strength God has placed in us to come under the control of the Holy Spirit, we are acknowledging the sovereign control of God over our lives. God's resources are ours as His Covenant sons and daughters.

Moses is described in the Bible as the most humble man in all the earth (see Num. 12:3). However, Moses stood before Pharaoh and spoke the word of the Lord in profound authority. He led a nation of several million out of captivity and through a 40-year journey in the wilderness. God manifested signs, wonders and miracles through him. Yet he is described as being humble above all other people.

WAITING ON GOD'S TIME

Submission is another positive response to the call of God, and that often requires patience. The Lord places leaders in the Body of Christ to help us grow into our destiny. As we allow these leaders to help steer us in our call, God will bring us into His revealed purpose for our lives.

I recall several times while my husband, Dale, and I pastored a local church when individuals would tell us about God's call on their lives. Frequently, after hearing the call, they would immediately want to rush into some type of "full-time ministry." They just knew God was calling them to quit jobs, often change locations, and be a pastor, prophet or evangelist overnight!

On one occasion we sat in our office with a couple, discussing their call. The couple had two children living at home and no car. Someone had promised to loan them a car to use with their travels. When we questioned them about the open doors for their ministry, they responded, "We don't have any open doors, but we know God will provide for us." No amount of reasoning could change their minds. They were determined to follow what they felt was the leading of the Lord.

A number of months later we saw the results of their lack of sub-mission to the leadership that God had placed in their lives. The couple ended up with no food, begging for handouts from people along the way. They spent their time living out of their borrowed car and going from town to town trying to get someone to allow them to min-ister. The family went through horrendous stress and difficulty that could have been avoided. God had given them a church with leadership who wanted to equip and send them out in strength, but they chose instead to run ahead of God's timing for their call. A submissive spirit will help avoid many casualties in life.

Why then, with all the wonderful plans God has for our lives, do some individuals choose disobedience to the call?

- Are these people rebellious?
- Is there sin operating in their lives?
- If someone rejects the call of God, does God give another opportunity to accept the call?
- Can emotional and social problems prevent a positive response to the call of God?

As an adult who finally came to understand that God had a call on my life, I remember my times of pleading with Him.

- Lord, You know I can't speak to people. If I speak to more than three people at one time, my voice closes off. I can't get one word out.
- Maybe You don't know enough good speakers. I will be happy to give You a lot of names. I'm sure they'll be glad to speak for You.
- Lord, I'm willing to move pianos, set up chairs and vacuum the floors for the meetings. I will do *anything* if You won't call me to speak.

You may have used some of the same reasoning with the Lord. Have you noticed He is not impressed? He wants our obedience, rather than our excuses and our attempts at bargaining.

Why did I, along with many others, choose a response of disobedience? Could it be that we all have areas in our lives we didn't know were there? Could it be that God is more interested in changing us than using us to change others? I believe so. At least, it has been that way for me.

FEARING GOD—OR FEARING MAN

While attending a conference shortly after comprehending my call, I heard a lady speaking. She made a statement that forever changed my life: "You will never walk in the fear of the Lord until you lose the fear of man." For the first time I knew there was a major problem in my life. It had always been there, but it was not until now that I could see it. *I had the fear of man operating in my life.* I cared more about what people thought about me than what God thought about me!

On the surface, the problem could not be seen. I was a faithful church member, involved in several Christian activities. My life seemed so together. My home and family were in order; my husband loved the Lord and was walking with Him; I prayed and studied the Bible on a daily basis. The problem had to do with motivation of the heart, rather than outward activities. The revelation of the fear of man in my life was overwhelming. How could I ever get rid of this horrible flaw in my character?

I remember lying on the floor in the conference and crying out to the Lord, "Please deliver me from the fear of man. More than anything else I want to walk in the fear of the Lord. I want to please You, rather than trying to please people." I didn't know how God would do this, but somehow I believed He would.

For a long time after that, each time I would have an opportunity to stand in front of people and speak, it felt like a claw gripped my throat. At those times I would hear the sweet voice of the Holy Spirit ask me a question: "Is this the fear of the Lord or the fear of man?" I knew each time I had to make a decision: To which fear was I going to yield? I remember responding to the Lord, "With Your help, Lord, I choose the fear of the Lord."

Somehow God gave me the grace to overcome the fear of man. The more I yielded to the fear of the Lord, the less of the fear of man I experienced. Today, I delight in God's call. He knew more about what would bring me fulfillment than I did. Now I can truly say along with David, "I delight to do Thy will, O my God; Thy Law is within my heart" (Ps. 40:8).

Moses had a similar problem. He did not want to receive God's call on his life because he had a problem speaking.

> Then Moses said to the LORD, "Please, Lord, I have never been eloquent, neither recently nor in time past, nor since Thou hast spoken to Thy servant; for I am slow of speech and slow of tongue." And the LORD said to him, "Who has made man's mouth? Or who makes him dumb or deaf, or seeing or blind? Is it not I, the LORD? Now then go, and I, even I, will be with your mouth, and teach you what you are to say" (Exod. 4:10-12).

God used Moses to speak to Pharaoh in Egypt and to deliver the Israelites from 400 years of captivity. He always gives grace to do what we cannot do in the natural. He is not looking for outstanding mouthpieces. He is looking for those who will allow Him to fill them with His ability.

> For consider your calling, brethren, that there were not many wise according to the flesh, not many mighty, not many noble; but God has chosen the foolish things of the world to shame the wise, and God has chosen the weak things of the world to shame the things which are strong, and the base things of the world and the despised, God has chosen, the things that are not, that He might nullify the things that are, that no man should boast before God (1 Cor. 1:26-29).

FEARING FAILURE

Fear of failure is another reason many people do not respond to God's call. Oftentimes we are afraid of that which we have not experienced. But fear not—the Lord loves to extend our perimeters! He loves to prove how powerful He is in the midst of inadequacy.

I remember a time shortly after I began speaking in churches and meetings. After driving to a meeting one night, I parked the car and reached to pick up my Bible and notes. As I reached for the notes, I heard the voice of the Lord: "Leave your notes in the car." I immediately replied, "I bind you, Devil. You will not put fear on me." You know what happened next; it has probably happened to you. "This is not the devil," the Lord countered. "This is the Lord. Leave your notes in the car."

I struggled with the Lord's command for about 30 minutes. Each time I would give in to the temptation of fear and reach to pick up the notes, the Lord would again instruct me to leave the notes in the car. I finally reached a place of courage and got out of the car. What happened next was a miracle!

Throughout the time I was speaking, the Lord said things through me that I had not thought about. These thoughts were not in my notes. God's power fell in the meeting that night. For the next one and a half years, the Lord did not allow me to use notes when ministering. I did not understand what He was doing at the time; today I do. He would have me study the Bible all week long. Then when I stood to speak, He would draw out of the deposit I had from the Word on the inside of me. I now understand that He was developing my prophetic ministry, but I did not know it at the time.

My reluctance to teach without notes was based on a fear of failure. I was fearful of not remembering what needed to be said and failing to deliver the fullness of the message. The Lord wanted me to see that He is able to hold me up and help me do what needs to be done. He is not looking for my ability. By leaning on Him, He will cause me to triumph in every situation.

> But thanks be to God, who always leads us in His triumph in Christ, and manifests through us the sweet aroma of the knowledge of Him in every place (2 Cor. 2:14).

GETTING A SECOND CHANCE FROM GOD

Entire books can be written on the many reasons a person fails to accept the call of God. Suffice it to say that all those whom the Lord has called can remember reasons they were hesitant to respond. Some people even think that their reluctance in the past prevents God from using them today. God is the God of the second chance, a God of redemption and restoration. If that were not the case, we would all be a people without hope. God's Word promises that He does not change His mind concerning His call.

> For the gifts and the calling of God are irrevocable (Rom. 11:29).

Allow the Lord to redeem the time in your life. Even though you may have taken some wrong paths, God knows how to get you back on His path. Let Him rekindle the fiery call He has for your life. May we be a people who not only hear the call of the Lord but who also respond, as did the prophet Isaiah.

Then I heard the voice of the Lord, saying, "Whom shall I send, and who will go for Us?" Then I said, "Here am I. Send me!" (Isa. 6:8).

THE REAL STORY
RESPONDING TO THE CALL IN MY LIFE
BELIEVING THE PROPHETS

Testimony by C. Peter Wagner
Cofounder of the World Prayer Center
Chancellor of the Wagner Leadership Institute,
Colorado Springs, Colorado

God's call can take many different forms, one of which is through prophecy. On June 6, 1998, God clearly called me through a prophecy. A group of friends were gathered in our living room that evening celebrating Chuck Pierce's birthday. Suddenly, Cindy Jacobs received a strong prophetic word for me, which we tape-recorded. She prophesied God would use me to start a new school for training leaders.

How did I respond to the call? First, I was totally perplexed, because I had never contemplated starting a school in my life. But, because I remembered that 2 Chronicles 20:20 said to believe the prophets, I began praying about it. A month later I resigned my position as a full-time Fuller Seminary faculty member. Then God began pouring revelation into my spirit concerning the shape that the school was to take. The next step was to implement what God had called me to do. Before the end of 1998, Wagner Leadership Institute was a reality.

The Bible promises that if we believe the prophets, we will prosper. This divine call caused me to begin a brand-new career at age 69. In all my years of ministry, I have never been happier, more fulfilled and as fruitful for the kingdom of God as I am now. I obeyed God's call, He kept His promise, and I am prospering!

DISCUSSION QUESTIONS

1. What are two responses that a person can have to the call of God?
2. Why is faith a necessary ingredient in vision?
3. Discuss your understanding of humility.
4. Is it possible to flow in the supernatural power of God and remain humble? Why or why not?
5. Why is sacrifice linked with humility?
6. Meekness is not _____.
7. Describe a picture of meekness.
8. Why do I need to submit to leaders when God has a call on my life?
9. What is the difference between the fear of the Lord and the fear of man?
10. Have you experienced the fear of man? If yes, how did you deal with it?
11. Describe several excuses that can hinder a person from accepting God's call.

Notes

1. John C. Maxwell, *The 21 Irrefutable Laws of Leadership* (Nashville, TN: Thomas Nelson, Inc., 1998), p. 189.
2. Doug Fortune, *Apostolic Reformation: In His Image* (McPherson, KS: Trumpet Call Publishing, 2001), pp. 94-95.
3. James Strong, *Strong's Concordance of the Bible, Hebrew and Caldee Dictionary* (McLean, VA: MacDonald Publishing Company, n.d.), p. 90.
4. W. E. Vine, *Vine's Expository Dictionary of New Testament Words* (McLean, VA: MacDonald Publishing Company, n.d.), p. 738.

GROWING IN THE CALL

The assignment was to write a story on any topic we chose. Although I was only 10, I clearly remember the teacher's instructions. How excited I was to be able to create a story of my own choosing, rather than writing on an assigned topic!

I have always enjoyed studying maps. As I gazed at the numerous countries on the large map on the wall, my finger fell on a particular nation, and I wondered what it was like to be a 10-year-old living there. That's when I knew exactly what I would write about.

After settling back into the seat at my desk, I began. As the story unfolded in my imagination and was transferred by pencil to the paper in front of me, I tried to put myself in the place of a child my age living in that foreign setting. Would I ever be able to visit such a place? This country seemed light-years away. How could I ever hope to travel that far? And why did I continue to think about that assignment so many years after it had been completed?

UNDERSTANDING AND FULFILLING THE VISION

Today, I realize the Lord was putting a vision in my heart that could not be removed. Sometimes we think certain situations are only childhood dreams. We chalk them up to fantasies or vivid imaginations. Yet God has a way of putting a seed of vision in us and causing it to grow until we fulfill that vision. And He has promised He would do that in our day.

It will come about after this that I will pour out My Spirit on all mankind; and your sons and daughters will prophesy, your old men will dream dreams, your young men will see visions. And even on the male and female servants I will pour out My Spirit in those days (Joel 2:28-29).

Vision is necessary as a person matures in the calling of God. The vision does not necessarily come through a supernatural encounter with the Lord. My vision came in the classroom as I simply released myself to see beyond where I was in the natural. However, vision sometimes comes in supernatural ways.

Throughout the Bible, many individuals received visions of their calling from the Lord. The apostle Peter received a vision from the Lord while on a housetop, praying. God was about to bring the Gentiles into the Body of Christ. He showed Peter how He would use him to open the door to the Church for people who were not already part of God's family.

While Peter was reflecting on the vision, the Spirit said to him, "Behold, three men are looking for you. But arise, go downstairs, and accompany them without misgivings; for I have sent them Myself" (Acts 10:19-20).

Some of the meanings of "vision" found in the dictionary are the following:

Something seen by other than normal sight; a mental image; esp. an imaginative contemplation; the ability to perceive something not actually visible, as through mental acuteness or keen foresight.[1]

Therefore, vision can come through a supernatural encounter with the Lord, or it can simply be a mental image of something for the future. How the Lord brings vision is really not the issue. How we allow the Lord to fulfill the vision is what is important.

Pastor Tim Sheets, in his book *Being Led by the Spirit,* tells how God communicated His call on Tim's life through visions. Sheets says that whenever he would be thinking or praying about what God had for his life, he would see himself standing before people and preaching.

These visions must have occurred dozens of times, and each time they did, something deep within would start doing flips. There would be a tremendous excitement down in my spirit and I would hear the Holy Spirit saying, "That's what you are supposed to do." What was happening? God was communicating His purpose for my life by using a vision.[2]

In many instances, circumstances make the vision seem impossible to fulfill. Faith is necessary to fulfill our call. Inadequacy and insecurity try to rob us of our destiny, but God has put a seed of faith in us. We simply have to water it and allow it to grow. Author Jay Blevins seems to agree:

The real issue is not faith, but exercising and expressing the measure you have, developing it unto perfection in Jesus. Because many of God's children are not able to walk in a certain area of faith, they get discouraged and say there is nothing to the faith walk. Saints, IT IS THE ONLY WALK WITH GOD. Do not be discouraged—just seek him more diligently from His Word and lay the promises in your heart, know His will. You will learn to exercise or release it as you grow up in your daily walk with God through Jesus Christ. All have to come the same way.[3]

Abraham is listed in the Faith Hall of Fame, found in the book of Hebrews. He was a man willing to obey in faith, although he did not fully understand where God was leading him.

By faith Abraham, when he was called, obeyed by going out to a place which he was to receive for an inheritance; and he went out, not knowing where he was going (Heb. 11:8).

Vision keeps us moving forward in the Lord's purposes.

Where there is no vision, the people perish (Prov. 29:18, *KJV*).

The word "vision" carries with it the idea of a prophetic revelation. God's purposes for the future are involved. We must know where the

Lord is taking us. Otherwise, merely living life and taking a lot of detours will cause us to miss our destiny.

The generation of Israelites who came out of Egypt missed their destiny. The Lord spoke of His plan to give them the Promised Land. Over and over He repeated His promise by saying, "I will."

> Say, therefore, to the sons of Israel, "I am the LORD, and *I will* bring you out from under the burdens of the Egyptians, and *I will* deliver you from their bondage. *I will* also redeem you with an outstretched arm and with great judgments. Then *I will* take you for My people, and *I will* be your God; and you shall know that I am the LORD your God, who brought you out from under the burdens of the Egyptians. And *I will* bring you to the land which I swore to give to Abraham, Isaac, and Jacob, and *I will* give it to you for a possession; I am the LORD" (Exod. 6:6-8, emphasis added).

Later, when Moses the prophet was on the mountain receiving the Law of God, no prophetic voice remained in their midst. The prophetic revelation of where God was taking them was forgotten. In other words, they lost their vision. When we don't have a vision, we go backwards—we perish. A prophetic revelation, or vision, will keep us moving forward toward God's destiny for our lives.

WRITING THE VISION

Time and again we observe families running in different directions. In the same way a church, ministry or individual needs a God-given vision, so do families. Families need to write the vision God has given them, so they know how to move forward together.

> Then the LORD answered me and said, "Record [write] the vision and inscribe it on tablets, that the one who reads it may run. For the vision is yet for the appointed time; it hastens toward the goal, and it will not fail. Though it tarries, wait for it; for it will certainly come, it will not delay" (Hab. 2:2-3).

The full picture of God's vision may not be in our lives instantly. Usually we begin to walk out the vision before we get further revelation.

Abraham took the first step in fulfilling God's call on his life when he left Ur of the Chaldeans. Then God started revealing the plan for his life.

> The LORD said to Abram, after Lot had separated from him, "Now lift up your eyes and look from the place where you are, northward and southward and eastward and westward; for all the land which you see, I will give it to you and to your descendants forever. I will make your descendants as the dust of the earth, so that if anyone can number the dust of the earth, then your descendants can also be numbered" (Gen. 13:14-16).

As Abraham continued walking in obedience, God continued to reveal His call to Abraham and blessed his life of faith. We need to respond to the Lord in faith, knowing He will bring us into the fullness of our call.

Frank Damazio says the same thing in his book *The Making of a Leader*:

> God did not reveal to Joshua the full extent of his ministry at one time. He revealed it to him gradually. We first saw Joshua as a warrior, then as a leader, then as a man who caused Israel to possess her inheritance, and now finally as the chief shepherd over the entire nation. God did not reveal the full extent of Joshua's ministry, because he might have destroyed both his life and his ministry by trying to help God fulfill it.
>
> Similarly, every leader should accept the progressive revelation of his ministry.[4]

BEGINNING SMALL

Many times I find people who are waiting for some fantastic door of opportunity to open before they are willing to step into their calling.

I encourage these people to do whatever their hands find to do. No great leader ever began at the top. Leaders begin the same way everyone else does: with small things.

I recently heard a story about a man named Jason who could not find a job. He applied for every position available. Because his situation was critical, he was willing to do anything, yet nothing opened up for him.

Jason really wanted to work for a company that did not have any openings. He went to the personnel manager and asked about volunteering his time for several hours each week. After being accepted for volunteer work, Jason set out to be the best employee in the company—without pay! Quickly people started recognizing the excellence in Jason's work. Before long, a position became available, and guess who got the job? Jason had proven himself to be a good worker, whether he was paid or not. As a Christian, he realized that his work was a reflection of the Lord Jesus. He wanted the name of the Lord to be honored through his life. Therefore, he tried to do the best job he was capable of doing. Jason is a living example of a wise servant.

The king's favor is toward a servant who acts wisely (Prov. 14:35).

Jason's excellent spirit did not stop when he became a paid employee. He continued to be faithful and to work in a spirit of excellence. Before long, Jason was part of the top leadership in that company. He started out doing whatever his hand found to do, and he did it as unto the Lord. The Lord in turn saw Jason's faithfulness and caused him to find favor. The favor of the Lord resulted in promotion and wealth.

Favor is not necessarily a free gift. In his dictionary Vine says:

Grace (*charis*—Gr.) implies more than favor and is a free gift. However, favor (*charitoo*—Gr.) may be deserved or gained.[5]

In other words, we can do certain things that bring God's favor into our lives. Jason was willing to sacrifice and live a godly life before his coworkers. God granted him favor. With favor came promotion and a place of greater influence for the Lord.

RECEIVING GOD'S FAVOR

When someone receives the favor of the Lord, it is important to remember why the favor is there. It is not because the person has arrived as some "supersaint." It is not because the person is perfect. One of the main reasons we receive the favor of the Lord is because He has a mission for us. We cannot complete the assignment He has for us without His favor resting upon us.

There are times when all our efforts seem to be in vain, when nothing we do will work. Although I am aware of the enemy and times of warfare, there is still another consideration. We may be trying to do something God has not favored us to do.

- Is there a "brick wall" that will not move?
- Have you prayed every prayer you know to pray?
- Is the timing of the Lord right for this task?
- Have you sought the counsel of more mature believers?
- Are you sure you have a word from the Lord concerning this task, or could it be a desire of your own?

God gives favor so that His assignments can be accomplished. Doors previously closed will open. Provision and resources for the vision are suddenly available. Increased numbers of people want to assist you in your God-given job. Favor rests upon you—favor to be successful in your calling from God. Without God's favor, our best efforts do not produce. Let the Lord direct you as you grow in your calling. One of the ways He directs is that He gives favor for you to be successful. As success comes your way, you realize this is not a result of your talented abilities. The Lord has made success possible. Therefore, He receives all glory and honor.

RECEIVING GOD'S POWER

Favor and empowering from the Lord are necessary ingredients to move forward in God's calling. Although I had been a Christian since the age of 12, I was powerless in my walk with the Lord. Fears, timidity and inadequacy seemed to cloak everything I attempted. Then, in 1974, I received the baptism of the Holy Spirit. My whole life was radically transformed!

My husband, Dale, had received the baptism of the Spirit two years prior, and he was so excited about Jesus. I thought he was just a fanatic. In fact, he was! He was fanatical about living a godly life and finding his whole purpose for living. Prayer and study of the Bible were constants for him. Meanwhile, I attended church but continued life as a relatively powerless Christian.

Immediately after receiving the Holy Spirit in fullness, I noticed an incredible hunger for God's Word. I also wanted to pray all the time. There was an increasing boldness that seemed to override all my fears and insecurities. Jesus promised this to those who were filled with His Holy Spirit.

> But you shall receive power when the Holy Spirit has come upon you; and you shall be My witnesses both in Jerusalem, and in all Judea and Samaria, and even to the remotest part of the earth (Acts 1:8).

The Holy Spirit gives the empowering for the work of the Lord. Abundant benefits are received from this empowering.

BENEFITING FROM THE HOLY SPIRIT

The first benefit of the Holy Spirit is that He gives us constant companionship, and He is our helper. He helps us do what we cannot do in the natural. I had never been able to pray for people and see them healed before receiving the Holy Spirit. Now, since I received the Holy Spirit, I could write several books about people who have been healed of medically incurable diseases.

> I will ask the Father, and He will give you another Helper, that
> He may be with you forever; that is the Spirit of truth, whom

the world cannot receive, because it does behold Him or know
Him, but you know Him because He abides with you, and will
be in you (John 14:16-17).

The Holy Spirit also gives the benefit of becoming our teacher.
Most people are looking for some formula, so they will not make a mis-
take. God has provided the Holy Spirit to teach us what to do in the
diverse circumstances we face.

As for you, the anointing which you received from Him abides
in you, and you have no need for anyone to teach you; but
as His anointing teaches you about all things, and is true and
is not a lie, and just as it has taught you, you abide in Him
(1 John 2:27).

The Holy Spirit does not invalidate human teachers. Ephesians
4:11-12 tells us that Jesus gave us teachers to equip us and bring us
into maturity. However, teachers are not with us all the time. They
can teach *principles,* but the Holy Spirit will teach us by revelation
how to *apply* those principles. He will give us the wisdom we need
that will supercede the wisdom of man. The Holy Spirit lives on the
inside of us and teaches us what to do when we do not know what to
do.

Another benefit of the Holy Spirit is that He interprets and gives
us understanding of the Scriptures. Before I was filled with the Spirit,
I could not understand the Bible. Even though I was a Christian and
in a church that taught the Bible, I did not understand most of what
I read. After receiving the Holy Spirit, the Scriptures came alive to me.
I saw and understood things I could not understand before. It was as
though I had a veil lifted from my eyes. Jesus promised that His Spirit
would bring understanding of the Scriptures to us.

But when He, the Spirit of truth, comes, He will guide you
into all the truth; for He will not speak on His own initiative,
but whatever He hears, He will speak; and He will disclose to
you what is to come (John 16:13).

A powerful benefit of the Holy Spirit is that He brings liberty. My true person was locked up in a prison of fear, timidity, insecurity and inadequacy. Jesus came to set us free. The Holy Spirit unlocks prison doors and releases us to fulfill our destiny. When I look back at myself so long ago, it is hard to comprehend that I was so bound. It seems as though I was a different person. And in reality, I was! The imprisoned person was not the genuine me. The power of the Holy Spirit unlocked all that was bound and released me to come into my destiny. I could not do what I am doing today without the work of the Holy Spirit inside me.

RECEIVING GOD'S SPIRIT

What the Lord through the power of the Holy Spirit did for me, He will do for you. What do you need to do to receive the Holy Spirit? First, repent of any sin that may be in your life.

> From that time Jesus began to preach and say, "Repent, for the kingdom of heaven is at hand" (Matt. 4:17).

After you have repented, receive cleansing from your sin. Do not allow the enemy to keep digging up old garbage that Jesus has washed away. Rejoice that you are not only forgiven but also cleansed.

After repentance, be sure you have received salvation. Eternal life is not based on any good works of man. It rests entirely upon faith in what Jesus did when He died, was buried, rose triumphantly from the grave and is now seated at the right hand of the Father. It is faith in what Jesus did, not what I did—or you did—that saves us. After receiving or reaffirming salvation, ask for Jesus to baptize you in His Holy Spirit.

> He said to them, "Did you receive the Holy Spirit when you believed?" And they said to him, "No, we have not even heard whether there is a Holy Spirit." And when Paul had laid his hands upon them, the Holy Spirit came on them, and they began speaking with tongues and prophesying (Acts 19:2,6).

As you hunger and thirst for more of the Lord, Jesus willingly fills you with His Holy Spirit. Ask for this gift from the Lord. The key to receiving anything from God is simply to accept it by faith. Ask and expect to receive.

> If you then, being evil, know how to give good gifts to your children, how much more shall your heavenly Father give the Holy Spirit to those who ask Him? (Luke 11:13).

The Holy Spirit will empower you to fulfill your God-given vision. Allow Him to cause you to grow in your calling. Expect great things from God. He loves to do *extraordinary* things through *ordinary* individuals!

THE REAL STORY
GROWING IN THE CALL
My Life Story

Testimony by Jim W. Goll
Cofounder, Ministry to the Nations, Antioch, Tennessee

I grew up in a little town of 259 people in Missouri, attended a Methodist church and loved the Lord with all my heart. Little did I know that years later, this same skinny kid would grow up to be an international minister, traveling the globe, fanning into a flame an insatiable desire for the presence of God. However, it has unfolded one step at a time.

Like others, I have had many opportunities to check out of the race along the way. Nevertheless, when the tough times come, instead of bailing out, I have chosen to embrace the Cross, keep looking to the author of my faith and just keep on going. Here are some practical points I have learned in life's journey:

1. Be faithful and He will reward you.
2. Seek the character to carry the gift.

3. Forgive often and bless others.
4. Learn from your mistakes and then get back up and go again.
5. Realize that He is on your side.

That's how it has worked with me, and I have a feeling that is how it will also work with you. When the tough times come, the resilient keep on going.

GROWING IN MY CALL

Testimony by Norma Anderson
Entrepreneur, Dallas, Texas
Volunteer, Wentroble Christian Ministries

In the early morning of May 15, 1975, the Lord touched my life. I then set out on a path to pursue my destiny. "There is an appointed time for everything" (Eccles. 3:1). Along the way, many quality people have helped me to mature in my calling:

- my parents, Lawrence and Alice Gorter, from whom I inherited many blessings
- my Faith Temple Church family in Sioux Falls, South Dakota, where I received an excellent foundation in the Word of God
- Dr. Freda Lindsay at Christ For the Nations, Inc., in Dallas was a powerful mentor. As manager of the editorial department for over five years, she not only was my direct supervisor but I also witnessed daily her strong faith and Christian walk
- Dr. Jim and Jean Hodges, who continually provide unwavering leadership, not only to me personally but also to my family

About 10 years ago I stepped into another aspect of my calling. I volunteered to help Wentroble Christian Ministries (WCM) with stuffing mail envelopes. I then offered to assist Dale and Barbara with proofreading and editing publications. Now Barbara is writing her fourth book. As I have volunteered and developed my call, I have watched the ministry of WCM increase in its call as well.

While growing in my call, I watched my only child, Melanie, become established in her faith and calling. In 1985 she graduated from Christ For the Nations Institute (CFNI). In 1996 she married Rev. Woodrow Blok, national of Sri Lanka and graduate of CFNI (1990). In Sri Lanka they have established a church, Bible school and children's ministry.

In addition, the books of Nehemiah and Ephesians have given me direction and guidance. They seem to speak to me in a personal way.

I thank the Lord for the many people who have touched my life. To me, the Christian life is fulfilling and rewarding. I have satisfaction knowing that I am growing in my call and fulfilling my destiny.

DISCUSSION QUESTIONS

1. Do you remember having a childhood dream about your future?
2. Do you still have it?
3. How are you walking out that dream?
4. What method did the Lord use to call you?
5. Describe the meaning of "vision."
6. What are some of the things that tend to rob us of our vision?
7. _____ will keep us moving forward toward God's destiny for our lives.
8. Can favor be earned or deserved?
9. Why do we need favor?
10. What are some of the benefits of the Holy Spirit?
11. Have you received the Holy Spirit since you believed?
12. Are you ready to pray, ask, believe and receive the Holy Spirit? If so, get ready for your life to be radically transformed!

Notes

1. *Webster's New World College Dictionary,* 4th ed., s.v. "vision."
2. Tim Sheets, *Being Led by the Spirit* (Middletown, OH: Tim Sheets, 1987), p. 111.
3. Jay Blevins, *Faith Must Be Developed* (Little Rock, AR: Jay Blevins Evangelistic Association, 1977), p. 13.
4. Frank Damazio, *The Making of a Leader* (Portland, OR: City Bible Publishing, 1988), p. 141.
5. W. E. Vine, *Vine's Expository Dictionary of New Testament Words* (McLean, VA: MacDonald Publishing Company, n.d.), p. 424.

CHAPTER 4

A Firm Foundation for the Call

I awakened with the dream still vivid before me. I had been walking through a house with uneven floors. There would be times when I was walking uphill, and then, within a few seconds, I was going downhill. The entire house seemed so unstable. After waking, I could not shake the dream. At times I know a dream is from the Lord. Other times I know it is only caused by something happening in my life. This dream I knew was from the Lord, yet I did not have the interpretation of it at the moment.

A couple of weeks later I was in my front yard, checking on the flower beds, when a next-door neighbor came over. "I have a lot of damage to the foundation of my house," she informed me. "There are large cracks in the walls, and I can't open several windows." I knew her house was only four years old, so I was shocked. How could her foundation be damaged when the house was practically new?

Several weeks later I returned from a trip and was entering my home with some friends when the same neighbor came over again. This was unusual, as our neighbors didn't normally visit with each other. For the most part, they kept to themselves, driving their cars into the garage when they came home and closing the door. They hired people to mow their lawns, so we seldom saw our neighbors outside. It was actually difficult to know who lived in the neighborhood. Still, this neighbor had come over to visit twice in a short time. When she did, she continued the story about her house.

"I have several thousand dollars' worth of damage to my house, due to the cracked foundation," she lamented. "That's not nearly as bad as some of these houses. Some people have had to move out. Huge holes have been drilled in the homes' foundations to put in extra support."

Suddenly, I remembered my dream. The house in my dream had uneven floors, giving it a sense of instability. Later, I was relieved to discover my own house was in good shape and had no damage to the foundation. But God used the dream to reveal a current situation and also to allow me to see what it is like when we do not have a firm foundation in our lives. The Bible describes believers as being the house of the Lord which must be built upon a firm foundation if it is going to stand in the day of storms.

> Therefore everyone who hears these words of Mine, and acts upon them, may be compared to a wise man, who built his house upon the rock. And the rain descended, and the floods came, and the winds blew, and burst against that house; and yet it did not fall, for it had been founded upon the rock (Matt. 7:24-25).

Without a proper foundation in our lives, the call of God can be delayed or even missed.

> If the foundations are destroyed, what can the righteous do? (Ps. 11:3).

HEARING GOD'S VOICE

For our foundation to be secure we must learn to hear the Lord and recognize His voice. God is our Father. As such, He desires to talk to His children. He is also a good shepherd. He has given us the ability as His sheep to hear His voice.

> My sheep hear My voice, and I know them, and they follow Me (John 10:27).

Throughout my walk in the calling of God, He has guided me with His voice. His voice will give direction and strength in the day of the storm.

The apostle Paul allowed God's voice to keep him from destruction when he was in a storm. In Acts 27 we read about Paul and some other prisoners being taken to Italy. Paul heard the Lord say the voyage would be accompanied by damage and great loss, including cargo, the ship and human lives. But the person in charge refused to accept Paul's words; he was determined to continue the voyage.

Later, as the ship was being tossed about in the midst of the storm, some of the sailors tried to escape and jump overboard. Paul gave instructions so that the sailors were unable to escape. He knew it was necessary for all to remain aboard if they were going to be safe. Paul encouraged the men to be courageous because he had heard from the Lord concerning their safety. The men listened to Paul and obeyed his word, and they reached the island of Malta in safety. Had they not obeyed the voice of the Lord spoken by Paul, lives would have been lost. Hearing and obeying the voice of the Lord will protect us in the day of storm and enable us to reach our God-given destination.

Learning to hear the voice of the Lord requires time spent alone with Him. In the midst of our busy lives, a discipline must be embraced and become as necessary and natural as breathing or eating. Learning to live by His proceeding word must become a way of life, not an option.

> But He answered and said, "It is written, 'Man shall not live on bread alone, but on every word that proceeds out of the mouth of God'" (Matt. 4:4).

Author Herman Riffel explains God's voice this way:

> The most basic requirement for hearing God's voice is finding the time to be alone with Him. The heart longs deeply for time to contemplate and meditate, which is the reason so many young people have sought out Eastern religions.
>
> There is a great difference, however, between the meditation of Eastern religions and that of Christianity. Eastern

religions call for the mind to become completely empty until it reaches a Nirvana stage of freedom from the external world. In Christianity, God calls upon us to become quiet until all the outer voices are stilled, so that we can hear him.[1]

COMMUNING WITH GOD IN PRAYER

We not only need to be able to hear God when He initially calls us, but we also need to be able to hear Him each step of the way as He leads us into the fullness of our calling. A vital part of our foundation is a life of prayer. Learning to hear God's voice is developed during these times of prayer. As we commune with Him, He communes with us. During this time of communion, we partner with the Lord to carry out His business here on Earth.

God is preparing His Church to reign with Him throughout all eternity. He uses prayer to prepare His Bride for her future role. God waits for man to pray, so He can release His will in the earth. Paul Billheimer emphasizes this in his book *Destined for the Throne*:

> His eternal purpose is the qualifying of His Eternal Companion for entering into full partnership with her Lord in the governing process of the universe. She can be qualified only through the apprenticeship of prayer and intercession. Only thus does she learn to enter into and participate in the eternal purpose of her Lord. Therefore, God will do nothing apart from His Church.

Billheimer goes on to quote E. M. Bounds:

> "The prayers of God's saints are the capital stock of heaven by which God carries on His great work upon earth. God conditions the very life and prosperity of His cause on prayer." If these things are true, then prayer should be the main business of our day.[2]

When I came into the fullness of the Holy Spirit, I possessed a deep desire for prayer. I remember the hours spent seeking the Lord and His will for my life. Sometimes I fasted while I prayed. I did not always understand why He called me to fasting and prayer; yet when I was obedient, I would see powerful results.

After one of these times of fasting and prayer, I was speaking at a meeting. A young man came up for ministry at the end of the meeting. "I need help," he pleaded. "I have so much fear in my life." Although I had never met the man, the Lord let me discern the cause of his fear. "Have you ever been involved in the occult?" I asked. After a positive response, I instructed him to wait until I finished praying for the others. Several ushers promised to stay close to him until I could finish ministering to those waiting for prayer.

Later, the Lord gloriously delivered this young man. The battle was strong, but the Lord was victorious. His brother-in-law later told me the man had only received Jesus a few weeks before. He had visited a pastor the preceding night. When the pastor began questioning him, the young man jumped up and ran out of the office. The torment kept him running from those who could help him. God used the time of fasting and prayer to equip me to set this captive free. Although I did not know I would face this situation during the time of fasting and prayer, the Lord knew.

> And he said unto them, "This kind can come forth by nothing,
> but by prayer and fasting" (Mark 9:29, *KJV*).

Years after praying for the young man in that meeting, someone informed me that after his deliverance, he joined a local church and became involved in Bible study. How thankful I was that the Lord led me to fast and pray before the meeting!

The Lord desires to release His will on the earth. He uses His people to help in this task. Prayer increases our sensitivity to the Lord's will. It also empowers us to do the Lord's bidding.

MEDITATING ON THE WRITTEN WORD OF GOD

Another vital part of our foundation for the call is the Word of God— the Scriptures. As a child in Sunday School, I did not understand why

I needed to read my Bible each day. I thought the only benefit I would receive was to get a check mark on my offering envelope, and that gave me 10 percent of the requirements needed for a total of 100 percent. It was easy to come to church on time, give an offering, listen to the pastor preach and do a few other required things. By performing those quick tasks, I could have a total of 90 percent marked off on my envelope. Why should I spend the entire week reading my Bible and only receive 10 percent? After all, 90 percent wasn't too bad! How little I understood the necessity of having a foundation built upon God's Word in my life.

With the baptism of the Holy Spirit came an intense hunger for God's Word. I spent hours each day reading and studying the Scriptures. The Bible came alive to me, and I saw and understood things I never had before. Although I had been in church all my life, I had never been able to comprehend the treasures found in the Word. Now I had an open treasure box with the riches of God available to me. How I loved it!

The enemy desires to keep us blinded to the life that is found in the Word of God. Ignorance of God's Word can keep us bound to darkness, misery and the power of sin. God desires to bring understanding and wisdom from His Word so we may no longer be slaves to the evil one but grow into sons and daughters of God who share in His inheritance. As we meditate on the Word of God, it becomes a lamp for our feet and a light for our path (see Ps. 119:105). We can stand strong in the Lord when our foundation is built upon God's Word.

BECOMING A WORSHIPER

Another aspect of our foundation is a life of worship. Many Bible scholars believe that at creation man was originally clothed like his maker in light and glory, made in the image and likeness of God (see Gen. 1:27). As a consequence of the Fall, man lost his original clothing. Due to the restoration purchased by Jesus through His death, burial, resurrection and ascension to the throne of God, we are now in a position to receive all that mankind lost in the Fall. God is restoring His people back into the image of God.

Restoration and transformation come as we enter into worship. Worship is not merely singing songs in a church service. I can remember singing from a hymnbook in church for many years. It seemed that we sang to give us something to do until the preacher was ready to preach. Although I was singing, I was not worshiping. Consequently, my life was not transformed as a result of the song service.

When I fell in love with Jesus, all that changed. I would find myself singing love songs to my Savior (even though I am certainly not musical). Somehow I realized He did not care whether I could carry a tune or not. He was interested in the expression of my heart.

One evening I attended a conference and joined the group as they sang a song I had learned as a child: "Jesus loves me this I know, for the Bible tells me so." I found myself pouring my heart of love out to the Lord. As we were singing, I saw something. Jesus was standing in the room. A little girl around four years old was running up to Him. She was dressed in a frilly white dress and wore a bow in her hair. As she got close to Jesus, He reached down and picked her up in His big strong arms. Those arms felt so safe and secure that her fears and insecurities seemed to drain out of her during His embrace. How good it was in His presence!

Later that evening I realized I was the little girl in the vision. I had never experienced anything like that before. After that, I began to notice a significant change in my life. Fears started disappearing. I felt more secure and confident than I had ever felt in my life. Friends started noticing the difference. As I continued my lifestyle of worship, Jesus continued to transform me. Through the years, I have realized that transformation does not come through focusing on my deficiencies and woundedness. Transformation comes as I focus on Him and His incredible love for me.

> But we all, with unveiled face beholding as in a mirror the glory
> of the Lord, are being transformed into the same image from
> glory to glory, just as from the Lord, the Spirit (2 Cor. 3:18).

As we behold the Lord in worship, He changes us so we can look like Him.

Judson Cornwall shows how this works in a negative way for those who worship false gods:

> To become conformed to the image of the object worshipped must be the end desire of the worshipper. These very aspirations cause his character to become more and more like his god. The history of idolatry gives ample proof of this. Consistently the character of every nation and tribe throughout the history of civilization has been molded and shaped by the character attributed to his or her gods. Indeed, man becomes like the object of his worship.[3]

Father God desires children who look like Him. Worship is an avenue God uses to restore His children into the image of the Father.

BEING SPIRITUAL PARENTS

In the Bible, believers are referred to as the family of God. The family unit consists of a father and a mother—spiritual parents. These parents are to help fashion the children into the people they were designed to be.

Too often today we come across believers who never knew what it was to have loving, affirming physical parents while they were growing up. As adults, they find themselves unsuccessfully trying to live the life described in the Bible. Some have had natural parents, but their parents were not Christians. Consequently, their core values are not in line with God's Word. Spiritual parents are vital to help fashion us as sons and daughters of God.

Jesus grew up in the home of Joseph and Mary. Joseph was a carpenter. We read of Jesus working in the carpenter shop. Joseph was training Jesus in the same skill that he possessed. The Lord desires His children to be trained in the skills and character He possesses. God uses parents to impart knowledge and skills to help children function successfully in the future.

I remember my husband, Dale, teaching our sons to change tires and to change the oil in their cars. Often, Brian and Mark were not interested in doing these chores. However, Dale insisted they learn these skills. "You never know when you will need to know how to do this," he insisted. Dale wanted to be sure his sons were prepared to handle these responsibilities if needed.

Spiritual parents help give direction and develop godly character in those God has assigned to them. These parents do not necessarily have to spend hours each day with those they are helping. It has been said, "Your actions speak so loudly, I can't hear what you're saying." The life of the parent speaks much louder than the words that are spoken.

God places people in our lives who love us enough to tell us the truth, even when we don't want to hear it. Many times these are the leaders God has given us. An independent spirit will prevent us from receiving from the leader the Lord has provided for us. We must see these leaders as gifts from the Lord and receive from them accordingly.

I remember a young lady who had a powerful prophetic call on her life, but she had started slipping into deception. Several reputable leaders visited with her, independent of one another, because each recognized this promising minister was in danger. Yet she dismissed all of them without having received their counsel.

I will never forget the time another minister friend and I went to the lady's house. We begged her to listen to us. She was incensed.

"How dare you question that I can hear God!" she retorted.

Sadness filled my heart as we drove from her house. The enemy had caused her to think she was okay, when she wasn't.

Years later I learned she continued in her deception. Eventually, she lost her husband, children, home, reputation and even soundness of mind. How different the story would have been had she listened to those God had placed in her life.

HAVING A SERVANT'S HEART

Finally, a good foundation is built on the heart of a servant. Servanthood will bring a person into greatness.

> But Jesus called them to Himself, and said, "You know that the rulers of the Gentiles lord it over them, and their great men

exercise authority over them. It is not so among you, but who-ever wishes to become great among you shall be your servant, and whoever wishes to be first among you shall be your slave; just as the Son of Man did not come to be served, but to serve, and to give His life a ransom for many" (Matt. 20:25-28).

It does not matter how lofty a position we may gain; in this life, we remain servants. Everything we do must be motivated by a heart to serve. If we lose this heart, then we should lock the door and shut down our endeavors. If anyone should have been served, it was Jesus; yet He chose to come as a servant. He is the example we follow.

As the Lord moves us forward in His call, we express His heart for people. We become His feet doing the will of the Father. We are His hands extended to those in need. May we be a people who build our house on a solid foundation. May we allow the Lord to transform us into His image so that when others see us, they will want to serve the same Jesus we serve.

THE REAL STORY
MOVING FORWARD IN HIS PLAN

Testimony by Robert D. Heidler
Senior Pastor, Glory of Zion Outreach Center, Denton, Texas

In 1983 I went through a "year from hell." Over the course of six months, I endured a painful kidney stone, bronchitis, strep throat and pneumonia. I was literally in bed most of the winter. I sought prayer and visited the doctor weekly, but nothing helped.

Because of my illnesses, I could not function as pastor. My church floundered. Medical bills devastated our finances. A deep and tangible depression settled over me. Finally, as I cried out to God, He asked, "If everything in your life falls apart, would you still love Me?"

That was a difficult question. I had devoted my life to God but felt He had abandoned me. Did I still *love* Him?

In response to His question, I thought about the many times of close fellowship I had enjoyed with Him. As I pondered these times, I realized I *did* still love Him, in spite of all that happened. I answered, "Yes, Lord, I still love You!"

A few days later the Spirit of God invaded our home in a powerful visitation. Depression was instantly broken and health restored. My whole life was put on a new path. God later showed me that He had given me a foundation, but it had to be tested. Only when I passed the test could He move me forward in His plan.

DISCUSSION QUESTIONS

1. Why is hearing the voice of the Lord an important part of the foundation in a believer's life?
2. Can you tell of a time when the voice of the Lord helped you through a difficult time?
3. How is prayer linked with God's will in the earth?
4. What are some of the consequences of being ignorant of God's Word?
5. _____ is an avenue God uses to restore his children into the image of the Father.
6. Why are spiritual parents important?
7. Who are some of the spiritual parents God has given you?
8. _____ brings a person into greatness.
9. Is your foundation solid? What are some weak areas you need to secure?
10. Isn't building a foundation an exciting adventure?

Notes

1. Herman Riffel, *Learning to Hear God's Voice* (Old Tappan, NJ: Chosen Books, 1986), p. 38.
2. Paul E. Billheimer, *Destined for the Throne* (Minneapolis, MN: Bethany House Publishers, 1975), p. 51.
3. Judson Cornwall, *Let Us Worship* (South Plainfield, NJ: Bridge Publishing, 1983), p. 160.

CHAPTER 5

CALLED TO DIFFERENT ARENAS OF LIFE

For the past number of years I've had the thrill and privilege of observing firsthand the Lord's healing power. Cancers and incurable blood diseases have been healed. Blind eyes have been opened. Broken bones have been mended and tumors have disappeared. I have discovered Jesus truly is the same yesterday, today and forever (see Heb. 13:8).

As I said before, I was instructed as a child that Jesus doesn't usually heal today, because you never know if it is His will to heal or not. He might heal on rare occasions, but that would not be the norm for today. When Jesus miraculously healed our youngest son, Mark, at age two, my theology about healing changed. Even the doctors acknowledged it was a miracle. After checking the Scriptures, I found that healing was purchased on the same Cross that bought eternal life for me (see Isa. 53:5).

EXPANDING THE VISION

For several years it was wonderful to witness the healing power of the Lord, as He brought wholeness to people. One day as I was walking through my house, I heard the Lord ask me, "Now that you have seen Me heal physical bodies, can you believe Me to heal cities and territories?" What a question! At that time I had never read books or heard teaching about the Lord healing geographical areas. This was an entirely new concept to me.

I knew the Lord was asking me to stretch my faith in a new way. He wanted me to believe Him to heal at a greater level than I had known in the past. From that day on, a burning desire came into my heart to see entire regions come into God's healing and restoration. My view of the world began to change. Up until that time, I realized I had embraced the same worldview many other Christians hold: Activities of the Church are spiritual; the secular world is carnal and separate from God. How wrong I was!

God intended for the entire world to enjoy His presence. When He created mankind, He put them in a garden. The garden was to be extended into the entire world. The inhabitants of the earth would then experience the presence and goodness of the Lord.

> Then God said, "Let Us make man in Our image, according to Our likeness; and let them rule over the fish of the sea and over the birds of the sky and over the cattle and over all the earth, and over every creeping thing that creeps on the earth." And God created man in His own image, in the image of God He created him; male and female He created them. And God blessed them; and God said to them, "Be fruitful and multiply, and fill the earth, and subdue it; and rule over the fish of the sea and over the birds of the sky and over every living thing that moves on the earth" (Gen. 1:26-28).

God's plan for man also included responsibility for the garden.

> Then the LORD God took the man and put him into the garden of Eden to cultivate it and keep it (Gen. 2:15).

The word "cultivate" in the Hebrew language is *abad*. Some of the meanings of abad are to work, to serve, or to plow. It also means to worship or to cause to worship.[1] God intended for man to work the garden. Work before the Fall was not unpleasant. Man was to plow and release worship in the garden.

I remember a few years ago when I was attending a meeting at Christian International in Florida. Around midnight Bishop Hamon sent for my husband and me, along with another couple, to come to his office. He called in a couple other prophets, and they prophesied over us. At the time he did not know me, and I had never met him.

"You are a caterpillar," he prophesied. "God is going to put all sorts of big batteries and cylinders on you," he continued, as I sat there thinking, *He considers me a little worm crawling on the ground.* Then, suddenly, I realized what he really meant. "Caterpillar" is a brand name for large earth-moving equipment—great big plows. Bishop Hamon was being absolutely scriptural in his prophetic utterance. God planned to send me to fields that needed me to plow up the ground. I liked that!

The Lord planned the same thing for each of us. He wants us to plow up the garden where He has placed us. Our garden may be our neighborhood. It may be our family. Our garden may be the place where we work or our city. As we plow the garden, something in our lives should cause everything in the garden to want to worship the same God we worship.

God also told man he was to *keep* the garden. The word "keep" in Hebrew is *shamar*, which means to restrain or keep within bounds, to hedge around something as with thorns, to watch as a watchman of sheep or cattle, to guard as a prophet.[2] In the garden, man was to keep such a careful watch that no evil thing could come into it. He was put as a protective hedge around the garden, so it would be a safe place.

The next responsibility man had in the garden was to rule. In the Hebrew language the word "rule" is *radah*, which means "to have dominion, to tread down as a winepress with the feet, to crumble." In the Talmud it means to take bread out of an oven. "Radah" also gives us a picture of taking possession of honey from a hive.[3]

Man's purpose in dominion was not *domination*. His purpose was *glorification*. He was to beautify the earth. God was giving man the authority to reach into the hot oven of the earth and pull out the fresh bread from heaven.

I have watched news reports on TV about those who withdraw honey from their beehives. They have an ability to go all the way through the mass of bees that have stingers. Without receiving personal injury, they take possession of the honey. God purposed for man to walk in this same authority against the enemy.

The next responsibility of man was to *subdue* the earth. The word "subdue" in Hebrew is *kabash*. It means "to trample, to conquer, to tread under the feet or to bring into subjection."[4] Joshua was told God would give him all the land where his feet would tread (see Josh. 1:3).

The final responsibility we find mentioned in God's plan for man is to *multiply*. "Multiply" in Hebrew is the word *rabah*. The meaning of "rabah" is to enlarge, to become many, much or great. It means wealth. "Rabah" comes from a primary word that means to shoot like an archer.[5] God's plan for man was that God's influence would multiply. His influence would be shot out to a far distance like an archer shoots an arrow. God's people would then become many. They would be people of wealth. Multiplication would be a result of radah and kabash.

RENEWING THE MANDATE

Although man failed in his responsibilities in the garden, Jesus came to restore all that was lost. Through faith in Him, man could once again gain the ability to fulfill God's original plan for his life. Jesus' Great Commission was a logical extension of God's original mandate to Adam in the Garden.

> And Jesus came up and spoke to them, saying, "All authority has been given to Me in heaven and on earth. Go therefore and make disciples of all the nations, baptizing them in the name of the Father and the Son and the Holy Spirit, teaching them to observe all that I commanded you; and lo, I am with you always, even to the end of the age" (Matt. 28:18-20).

How sad that the Church, in general, has failed to remember this mandate. Religion confined Christianity to our own private "prayer closet" or to a building we call "church." As a result of our failing to be an influence in our place of work—or to guard, watch over, rule and set a hedge around our garden—we have not multiplied in the way God intended. The Church has not been able to reach into the fiery hives of life and take possession of the sweet honey in the earth for the Lord.

Today in our society we find the very foundations of our Western thinking are crumbling. People are turning to New Age beliefs, Eastern religions and cults. Much of our society is involved in immorality and drugs. Sadly, the present-day Church has not been able to give an answer or be relevant to the needs of people in our modern world. According to George Barna, in a typical week, 41 percent of adults attending church are not even born again.[6] Desperately, we, the Church, need to return to a biblical worldview and receive the mandate found in Genesis and Matthew!

TRANSCENDING CONFLICTING WORLDVIEWS

The ancient Greek worldview was different from the Hebrew worldview. The Greek worldview divided the spiritual realm from the created realm. Their vision of reality was that church—or religion—was something separate from life and work. Plato taught that the created world around us was not actually the real world. The ideal world was in the eternal and detached from the temporal. This idealism can only be known vaguely, he professed, through concepts and, possibly, after death. As this thought entered the Church, a mind-set developed that separated God and the world.

Man saw himself as having to exist in a world separated from God, longing for the time he could be in church and learn about the real world he might enjoy someday. He sang songs about the sweet by-and-by. There was a longing for this real world called heaven. The focus was on a place that could only be hoped for and on a desire to escape the created world.

The Hebrew worldview was totally different. The Hebrews believed the spiritual, or unseen, world was in union with the created realm. Creation did not exist in a separate, or removed, dimension because God did not intend for there to be a distinction between divine things and natural things. All created things were intended to express and manifest the attributes, nature and power of the Son of God.

For by Him all things were created, both in the heavens and on earth, visible and invisible, whether thrones or dominions or rulers or authorities—all things have been created by Him and for Him (Col. 1:16).

Man was to mature in his revelation of the attributes, nature and power of God as he discovered God through every created thing. The Hebrews knew if man failed to see and encounter God in all of creation, man would then invite an idol to fill the vacuum. This vacuum in humanity has been filled with false religions, cults, occultic activity, humanism and all sorts of evil.

God's purpose for man was to enter into his role to rule over all creation. God was not to be confined to a certain place or activity. Man was to see God everywhere at all times.

O LORD, our Lord, how majestic is Thy name in all the earth, who hast displayed Thy splendor above the heavens! From the mouth of infants and nursing babes Thou hast established strength because of Thine adversaries, to make the enemy and the revengeful cease. When I consider Thy heavens, the work of Thy fingers, the moon and the stars, which Thou hast ordained; what is man, that Thou dost take thought of him? And the son of man, that Thou dost care for him? Yet Thou hast made him a little lower than God, and dost crown him with glory and majesty! Thou dost make him to rule over the works of Thy hands; Thou hast put all things under his feet, all sheep and oxen, and also the beasts of the field, the birds of the heavens, and the fish of the sea, whatever passes through the paths of the seas. O LORD, our Lord, how majestic is Thy name in all the earth! (Ps. 8).

FULFILLING OUR ROLES AS GOD'S IMAGE BEARERS

Man was made a little lower than God. He was to be the image bearer of the Lord. As God's image bearer, he was also to be God's manager, or steward, in the earth. The word "steward" means a person put in charge of the affairs of a large household or estate; one who acts as a supervisor or administrator, as of finances and property for another or other; a person morally responsible for the careful use of money, time, talents, or other resources.[7]

Man was put in charge of God's estate called Earth. He was morally responsible for his God-given talents, land, finances and everything pertaining to the created world. Good works of God's people were to shine forth the light of Jesus to a dark, futile world. These image bearers of the Lord were to fill the earth with the glory of God.

Arise, shine; for your light has come, and the glory of the LORD has risen upon you. For behold, darkness will cover the earth, and deep darkness the peoples; but the LORD will rise upon you, and His glory will appear upon you. And nations will come to your light, and kings to the brightness of your rising (Isa. 60:1-3).

Rather than the good works of man being done only in a church building, God intended them to be accomplished throughout all of society. Most of Jesus' works were achieved outside buildings of corporate worship. He is the example we are to follow. In fact, most of the good works carried out by people mentioned in the Bible were outside church or temple walls. These people were called to different arenas of life. However, they understood their purpose in life was to bring restoration and transformation into the *garden* God had placed them in. A few of the biblical people God used were the following:

- Joseph, who became a ruler under Pharaoh in Egypt, was used to save a nation, as well as his own family, from a famine: "You shall be over my house, and according to your command all my people shall do homage; only in the throne I will be greater than you" (Gen. 41:40).
- Bezalel, a craftsman, was used in the building of the Tabernacle of Moses: "And He has filled him with the Spirit of God, in

wisdom, in understanding and in knowledge and in all crafts-manship" (Exod. 35:31).

- Amos, a shepherd, prophesied to God's people about the coming judgment: "The words of Amos, who was among the sheepherders from Tekoa, which he envisioned in visions concerning Israel in the days of Uzziah king of Judah, and in the days of Jeroboam son of Joash, king of Israel, two years before the earthquake" (Amos 1:1).
- Luke was a physician and a writer: "Luke, the beloved physician, sends you his greetings, and also Demas" (Col. 4:14). "It seemed fitting for me as well, having investigated everything carefully from the beginning, to write it out for you in consecutive order, most excellent Theophilus" (Luke 1:3).

Many today in the Church are realizing that God wants to use them wherever they are. They are called to diverse functions in life. One function is not more spiritual than another. A preacher is not more spiritual than a dentist, carpenter or engineer. God calls people to different "gardens" to fulfill His mandate.

My husband is an engineer and functions as a manufacturing manager. He works directly under the corporate president who lives in Japan. Recently a supervisor in the plant told Dale about a problem with her hand. She could not close it, and she was experiencing a lot of pain. Several coworkers were concerned about her problem. The supervisor had come to know Jesus in the last couple of years, as Dale had witnessed to her. When Dale asked this lady if he could pray for her hand, she agreed; and he prayed a simple prayer, asking Jesus to heal her.

A few hours later the supervisor noticed the lady could close her hand, and she told him the pain had vanished. Several people in the plant also noticed the change in her hand. She was then able to tell them about the healing power of Jesus. Jesus was not confined to a church building. He was in the midst of a manufacturing plant. Dale and the supervisor were God's image bearers in that *garden*. God's glory is to be manifest through His people who work and live in the earth.

DOING BUSINESS UNTIL HE COMES

The Early Church comprehended the calling to extend God's purposes in the earth. Peter and John were God's image bearers. They understood their authority to rule over sickness and disease in the earth. One day a man born lame begged for money as they were walking to a prayer meeting. The healing power of God was manifest outside a church building when Peter spoke the name of Jesus and the lame man was healed at the Beautiful Gate (see Acts 3:1-10).

Our dear friends, Drs. Mark and Betsy Neuenschwander, are both physicians and founders of International Health Services Foundation. One of their functions is to train and equip people for disaster relief. The purpose behind the help given in times of crisis is evangelism and church planting. Although they are physicians, they understand their role is to bring restoration and transformation to the earth. Times of crisis open the doors for them to impact nations and people groups. Mark and Betsy have a call from God to use their skills for releasing God's light and glory to hurting, broken people in the nations of the world.

Rather than looking to escape from this world, believers today are waking up and responding to God's call in various arenas of life. Jesus did not tell His followers to try to escape this world. He told them to occupy it (do business) until He comes (see Luke 19:13).

God's image bearers are filling the earth with the glory of God. They will show people how good God is by demonstrating how life and work flow together. Image bearers will see the place God has put them as their mission field. Work will no longer be seen as a secular place among evil people. Occupations will be spiritual gifts given to strategically position God's people where they can release the power and life of the Spirit.

I pray we will become a people who respond to the call of God in whatever arena of life we are placed. No longer will we dream of the day we can quit our jobs and go into "full-time ministry." We will embrace the present moment and see the Lord's purpose for our current position. Even as Jesus said He must be about the Father's business at an early age (see Luke 2:49), we also must be about His business today, not just in some distant future.

We must work the works of Him who sent Me, as long as it is day; night is coming, when no man can work (John 9:4).

THE REAL STORY
My Call to a Different Arena of Life

Testimony by Brian Wentroble
Project Manager/Consultant, Software Development Company,
Dallas, Texas
Son of Dale and Barbara Wentroble

At the age of 18, I felt the pull of the Holy Spirit within me. I interpreted this as the Lord sending me into ministry. Having absolutely no desire to pastor a church, I figured I would become a music minister.

I spent the next two years in college as a music major, somehow trying to envision spending the rest of my life in church services. But I found I preferred the *Wall Street Journal* far above studying music. I didn't know that you could love Jesus with all of your heart while working in the business world. However, I finally came to understand that business was the only place I would be satisfied. I believed the Lord was telling me to trust that He had put the desires in my heart toward business.

Today my job in managing and balancing business decisions enhances my desire to seek the Lord daily in prayer. I'm working with people who will never hear the gospel in a church, but they will hear it from me. I'm sharing with them that God has a purpose and plan for their lives; I'm speaking prophetically into their lives; I'm trying to open their eyes to the miraculous. Being in the marketplace is exactly where the Lord wants me to be. I'm fulfilled in my destiny in the kingdom of God by doing His will in business.

DISCUSSION QUESTIONS

1. What does the word "cultivate" mean in a biblical sense?
2. What are some of the aspects of keeping the garden?
3. Describe one picture of ruling.
4. Man's purpose in dominion was not _____, but it was _____.
5. Multiplication was to be a result of two Greek words. If we are to multiply, we must _____ and _____.
6. Describe the Greek worldview.
7. _____ taught that the created world was not the real world.
8. How was the Hebrew worldview different from the Greek worldview?
9. Man, who was created a little lower than God, was to be His_____ _____.
10. What is a steward?
11. Name a Bible character who was used powerfully by God outside a church building.

Notes

1. Spiros Zodhiates, *The Hebrew Greek Key Study Bible: Lexical Aids to the Old Testament, New American Standard* ed. (La Habra, CA: AMG Publishers, 1990), p. 1755.
2. Ibid., ref. no. 8104.
3. Ibid., pp. 1774-1775.
4. James Strong, *Strong's Exhaustive Concordance of the Bible, Hebrew and Chaldee Dictionary* (McLean, VA: MacDonald Publishing Company, n.d.), p. 54.
5. Logos Library System, *New American Standard Hebrew-Aramaic and Greek Dictionaries* (La Habra, CA: Lockman Foundation, 1998), p. 725a.
6. George Barna quoted in Tim Ellsworth, "Baptists Adrift in Doctrinal Confusion," *SBC Life*, October 2001. http://www.sbclife.org (accessed December 10, 2001).
7. *Webster's New World College Dictionary*, 4th ed., s.v. "steward."

SECTION 11

THE CHOSEN

Behold, I have refined thee, but not with silver;
I have chosen thee in the furnace of affliction.

ISAIAH 48:10, *KJV*

CHAPTER 6

WHY IS ALL THIS HAPPENING?

The couple sat across the desk from Dale and me as they continued their line of reasoning with us. We had been talking for about one hour. Dale and I were pastors of the church this couple attended. Over the past several months we had seen a strong spiritual battle being waged against our congregation. The church was located in an area that has been described by many through the years as "the graveyard of preachers."

More than a few new works would begin in that area within a given month. Then an equal number of churches would close their doors within the same amount of time. I was teaching our intercessors on spiritual warfare and God's mandate to see our area brought into its God-given destiny. At that time not much was taught on this subject, and most believers in our area did not understand the concept.

As the intercessors started applying the principles being taught, it was as if war had broken out. Sickness, loss of jobs and discontented believers were only a few of the problems that surfaced. It seemed the more we prayed, the worse things got.

Now we were dealing with this couple who couldn't understand what was happening. They had not been part of the intercessory prayer group but wanted to express their concern. "We've been watching you," they said. "There must be sin in your lives. We have been looking but have not been able to find it. It must be there though. Otherwise, why would all this be happening to you?"

We sat there amazed at what we had just heard. Although we did not view ourselves as perfect, our lives had been an open book for all to see. We had walked with this couple through their own difficulties.

Our reputation in the community and among other pastors was without blemish. Why would they think there was some hidden sin in our lives? Why did they believe that if a person walks in the will of God, there would be no hard places?

SPIRITUAL WARFARE

Apparently the question asked us that day in our office was not a new one. Gideon wondered the same thing. When it was time for harvest, the Midianites came along with the Amalekites to destroy the crops of Israel. One day an Israelite named Gideon was hiding from the enemy in a winepress. He hoped for safety in this place and was busy beating out the wheat. Suddenly, Gideon saw an angel of the Lord.

> Then Gideon said to him, "O my lord, if the LORD is with us, why then has all this happened to us? And where are all His miracles which our fathers told us about, saying, 'Did not the LORD bring us up from Egypt?' But now the LORD has abandoned us and given us into the hand of Midian" (Judg. 6:13).

The couple in our office was using the same logic and asking the same questions as Gideon; they were not alone in their belief system. Many, in fact, believe that God's will for their lives comes to them wrapped in comfort. They believe God is a good God, but they don't believe there is a real enemy called Satan. George Barna stated that one Gallup survey revealed that 60 percent of Americans believe Satan is not a living being but just a symbol of evil.[1] The Bible, however, gives us a very different picture of the enemy.

> Be of sober spirit, be on the alert. Your adversary, the devil, prowls about like a roaring lion, seeking someone to devour (1 Pet. 5:8).

As we move forward in God's purposes, more often than not we meet with resistance. To be successful in our call, we must understand war. Old mind-sets sometimes have to be broken before the Lord can bring us into new revelation. Today, God is uncovering revelation found in the Word but not understood by many in our generation. One of the recent truths God has been revealing is in the topic of spiritual warfare.

The Bible has much to say about this warfare. War finds its beginnings in the first book of the Bible. I like the way the Bible begins: "In the beginning God" (Gen. 1:1). All there was in the beginning was God. Later the Lord created the heavenly beings called angels, the earth, mankind and all that is in the earth. One of the angels of heaven, whose Latin name was Lucifer, was the anointed cherub. Many believe he was the worship leader of heaven. The Bible describes Lucifer as a perfect creature until he tried to exalt himself above God. He wanted the worship that belonged to God alone.

At that time Lucifer became the first apostate. In his insubordination, he led one-third of the angels in rebellion against God. Up until then, there had been only one Kingdom—God's kingdom, the kingdom of light. When an evil rebellion occurred with Lucifer and his followers, a second kingdom came into existence. This kingdom is the kingdom of darkness. Lucifer and his evil angels were then cast out of heaven (see Ezek. 28:1-19; Isa. 14:4-23). From that moment forward, a battle has been raging between the two kingdoms.

There are vast differences between these two kingdoms.

__God's Kingdom__	__Satan's Kingdom__
Light	Darkness
Holiness and righteousness	Sin and unrighteousness
Healing and health	Sickness and disease
Truth	Deception
Joy and life	Sorrow and death

God created man and gave him the responsibility of ruling over the powers of darkness in the earth.

The heavens are the heavens of the LORD, but the earth He has given to the sons of men (Ps. 115:16).

Man failed in his responsibility in his garden, the earth. Man's failure did not take God by surprise. He had already planned for Jesus to redeem and restore man back to his original purpose. Part of our salvation includes all the above-mentioned distinctives of God's kingdom. Believers now have the authority and power to overcome the power of the enemy.

> Behold, I have given you authority to tread on serpents and scorpions, and over all the power of the enemy, and nothing shall injure you (Luke 10:19).

The enemy, however, tries to stop man from enjoying the blessings of this Kingdom. Although the enemy still has *power*, he does not have *authority*. The Church has been given the authority to be victorious over the plans of the enemy.

> In order that the manifold wisdom of God might now be made known through the church to the rulers and the authorities in the heavenly places (Eph. 3:10).

BROKEN RELATIONSHIPS

The enemy comes in several ways to hinder us from fulfilling God's call on our lives. The first way is through broken relationships. He is always seeking to break up relationships between man and God and between man and his family, friends or leaders. The enemy understands the power of unity and the damage that unity can bring to his kingdom.

> Again I say to you, that if two of you agree on earth about anything that they may ask, it shall be done for them by My Father who is in heaven (Matt. 18:19).

Hector Torres describes the way the enemy works to break up relationships.

Jealousy, envy, and the spirit of accusation are the greatest weapons for division. The enemy uses this spirit of accusation to bring discord, division, and doubt against our leaders and brothers. When this happens we can be sure it is not from God. God is not the author of confusion, but of peace. Satan can use holy vessels to interfere with God's plan.[2]

Christians are not called to compromise their convictions. However, *we can be so right that we are wrong.* A religious, legalistic attitude is just as wrong as any other sin. We are to walk in humility and a spirit of peace as we serve the Lord. We do this by recognizing when the enemy is trying to bring division, as well as by seeking to bring peace and reconciliation in God-given relationships.

Be angry, and yet do not sin; do not let the sun go down on your anger (Eph. 4:26).

HINDRANCES TO OUR MINISTRY

The enemy also comes to hinder God's call by trying to keep us from fulfilling the ministry of the Lord. In the Bible we see where the apostle Paul was hindered in carrying out the Lord's call on his life.

For we wanted to come to you—I, Paul, more than once—and yet Satan thwarted us (1 Thess. 2:18).

For this reason I have often been hindered from coming to you (Rom. 15:22).

When there is a hindrance, be sure you know the will of the Lord. God is not going to try to stop you from being obedient to His plan. That would be contrary to His nature. When you know it is the will of God, you will have courage to press through the obstacles.

The Lord had spoken His promise to the Israelites many times. When it came time for Joshua to lead them across the Jordan into the

Promised Land, they were instructed repeatedly to be very courageous. The Lord knew the enemy would try to hinder Joshua in God's plan for Israel. They would need courage to be obedient and resist fear. God promised that as they moved forward in His plan, He would be with them.

> Have I not commanded you? Be strong and courageous! Do not tremble or be dismayed, for the LORD your God is with you wherever you go (Josh. 1:9).

> As God was with Joshua, so He will be with you!

SICKNESS AND DISEASE

Another way the enemy seeks to hinder us from fulfilling God's call is through sickness and disease. Someone who is sick is not necessarily demonized. However, the enemy uses infirmity to hinder us. God is a healing Lord. Included in our salvation is healing—body, soul and spirit. Sometimes, however, the enemy is responsible for a person's sickness.

> And one of the crowd answered Him, "Teacher, I brought You my son, possessed with a spirit which makes him mute. And when Jesus saw that a crowd was rapidly gathering, He rebuked the unclean spirit, saying to it, "You deaf and dumb spirit, I command you, come out of him and do not enter him again" (Mark 9:17,25).

Another Scripture showing the enemy linked to sickness is found in the Gospel of Luke.

> And behold, there was a woman who for eighteen years had had a sickness caused by a spirit; and she was bent double, and could not straighten up at all. And when Jesus saw her, He called her over and said to her, "Woman, you are freed

from your sickness." And He laid His hands upon her; and immediately she was made erect again, and began glorifying God (Luke 13:11-13).

When a person is sick or battling an infirmity, find someone to pray who believes in the healing power of Jesus. Don't ask a person to pray who is not confident of Jesus' will and desire to heal.

Is anyone among you sick? Let him call for the elders of the church, and let them pray over him, anointing him with oil in the name of the Lord; and the prayer offered in faith will restore the one who is sick, and the Lord will raise him up, and if he has committed sins, they will be forgiven him (Jas. 5:14-15).

FALSE TEACHINGS

People can also be hindered in their call by receiving false teachings given by the enemy.

But the Spirit explicitly says that in later times some will fall away from the faith, paying attention to deceitful spirits and doctrines of demons (1 Tim. 4:1).

Doctrines are teachings. The Scripture warns believers against teachings that are given by demon spirits. These evil spirits give doctrines to teachers to promote their demonic work. They go about this by enticing preachers or teachers to taint their teachings by adding or subtracting from the truth.

These evil spirits use several methods to do their work. Some of them are

- giving their teachings to those who accept everything supernatural as being from God;
- making people believe they are not supposed to judge anything;

- convincing people that teachers of good character need not have their doctrine subjected to scrutiny;
- mixing their teachings with man's own reasonings so that people will conclude that the demon's thoughts are actually their own.

All teachings, revelations and prophecies are to be tested by the Word of God and the discerning of spirits.

Beloved, do not believe every spirit, but test the spirits to see whether they are from God; because many false prophets have gone out into the world (1 John 4:1).

KNOWING THE GOD OF VICTORY

In the midst of warfare we must know the enemy, but we must also know God. God plans for His people to walk in victory and not defeat, even in the midst of warfare. We can allow the warfare to make us *better*, or it can cause us to become *bitter*. Dean Sherman addresses this topic in his book *Spiritual Warfare for Every Christian*.

God uses evil in the world to develop us in two ways: first, as a battlefield in our lives. God doesn't intend for us to be casualties by becoming confused, angry, or resentful. Neither does He want us to hide our heads in the sand and pretend evil isn't all around us. He wants us to allow what is taking place on this planet to develop our lives, without letting it overtake us. The world is what it is, and the choice is ours. We can either let it strengthen us and increase our resolve to make a difference in the world, or we can let it weaken us and become a casualty of the war.[3]

In the Bible, we see David as a warrior. Frequently, he faced the attacks of the enemy. We sometimes think the people in the Bible were "supersaints." It can be difficult to view them as having the same feelings and emotions that we have. Nevertheless, God constantly has chosen to use ordinary people for His purposes. David was such an individual. According to historical records, David became discouraged due to the insurmountable battle he faced.

When David and his men arrived at a place called Ziklag, the city had been burned with fire. The enemy had taken captive the wives and children of David and his men. David and the men with him lifted their voices and cried until there was no strength left in them.

David experienced suffering and misery knowing his family had been taken captive. He witnessed the distress of his men. As if that weren't enough, his own men turned on him. They had become bitter in the battle and spoke of stoning David. At times it seems there is not a friend to be found in the midst of warfare.

In spite of the overpowering obstructions, David was an overcomer. He knew his source of strength. David was called to serve the purposes of God in his generation (see Acts 13:36). He did what we are all called to do in the midst of difficulty: David encouraged himself in the Lord:

> But David strengthened himself in the LORD his God (1 Sam. 30:6).

THE CALL AND THE VICTORY

Many times we must stir up the call of God and the gifts of God within ourselves (see 1 Tim. 1:18; 2 Tim. 1:6). One of the things I do in times of battle is review the prophecies that have been spoken over me. God has made promises for my life. I have purposes not yet fulfilled. He has a call that is not yet completed. Therefore, I remind myself that God, not the circumstances that seem to surround me, is in charge of my life.

My husband, Dale, says his favorite verse in the Bible is, "It came to pass" (Gen. 30:41, *KJV*). He also enjoys announcing, "That means it didn't come to stay."

Whatever battle you are in is only temporary; it is not permanent. Our future is in the Lord. God has promised to give us a hope and a future (see Jer. 29:11). In the darkest hour we can remind ourselves of God's plan for our future and draw hope from His promises.

Another thing I do in battle is to find someone who needs ministry, even though it is often the last thing I want to do. But other people are going through harder things than we are. The enemy, as well as our emotions, will try to convince us that *we* are the one in need, not others. However, allowing the gifts God has put in us to touch other lives will bring encouragement to us.

It is amazing that in times of weakness God loves to show how powerful He is. Some of the most powerful things the Lord has done through me have been when I felt the most inadequate. That is because, in those times, we tend to lean on His strength and not our own abilities.

In warfare we must not give up but press on in God's call. He has destined us for victory.

> The devil gets away with whatever we let him. This does not mean that he will give up easily. He knows human nature and is relying on our lack of endurance, hoping we will give up first, as we often do. If we continue to resist him he will finally give up. It may not be immediate, but it will happen. The more determined we are the less determined he is. If we are convinced that we have the authority, he will see it and eventually cease his attack. We should never give in or become discouraged. Victory is ours, but the price is faith and persistence.[4]

To be victorious in warfare, we must allow the Lord to change some of our old mind-sets. The Christian walk is not free from the fiery darts of the enemy. We must not be like the couple who thought that the enemy only attacks those who are walking in disobedience to the Lord. Our battle is with Satan's kingdom. In the midst of the battle we can be assured that we are on the winning side. The Lord has promised that we are going to see that "the kingdom of the world has become the kingdom of our Lord and of His Christ; and He will reign forever and ever" (Rev. 11:15).

THE REAL STORY
TREASURES OF DARKNESS

Testimony by Ruthanne Garlock
Popular author, editor, Bible teacher, retreat and seminar speaker
Garlock Ministries, Bulverde, Texas

With the author's permission, the following story has been adapted from
A Woman's Guide to Spiritual Warfare.[5]

During a difficult period in my life, I developed the habit of walking a mile every day to talk to the Lord and settle my thoughts. I was dealing with a rebellious teenager, caring for my invalid in-laws living in our home and trying to cope with financial pressures and myriad problems while my husband traveled frequently in ministry. I struggled against self-pity and the feeling that I was shouldering the load alone.

On my walk one crisp October morning the Lord spoke to me through this verse:

I will give you the treasures of darkness, and hidden wealth of secret places, in order that you may know that it is I, the LORD, the God of Israel, who calls you by your name (Isa. 45:3).

Then He said very clearly, "These are precious days. I am teaching you the treasures of darkness." I desperately wanted God to quickly solve all these problems—they certainly didn't seem "precious" to my natural mind—yet I knew they weren't going to evaporate overnight. The Lord said He was teaching me as I allowed Him to—there was value in the experience.

After that morning with the Lord, my circumstances actually got worse, not better. But I began to see that from God's point of view, my response to the difficulties was more important than the problems themselves. He obviously wanted to change me, and I finally consented.

I've come to believe that God does His best work in darkness: in creation, in the incarnation, in Gethsemane, at Calvary, in my own dark night of the soul. The glory of it all was not just seeing circumstances change—they eventually did. The greater blessing was allowing God to change me, and in the process coming to know God and His character in ways only adversity can teach.

DISCUSSION QUESTIONS

1. For the believer to be successful in his call he must understand _____.
2. What are the two kingdoms that are at war?
3. Describe the kingdom of God and the kingdom of Satan.
4. The enemy has _____, but he does not have _____.
5. What are some of the ways the enemy comes to break relationships?
6. Can the enemy hinder you from being obedient to God's call on your life? If so, how?
7. What is a characteristic a person needs to develop in order to press forward into God's call?
8. How can sickness and infirmity hinder you in your call?
9. What are doctrines? How do evil spirits give false teachings to teachers and preachers?
10. What kinds of people are susceptible to false teachings?
11. How do we encourage ourselves in the Lord?

Notes
1. George Barna, *The Second Coming of the Church* (Nashville, TN: Word Publishing, 1998), p. 21.
2. Hector P. Torres, *Pulling Down Strongholds* (Colorado Springs, CO: Wagner Institute for Practical Ministry, 1999), p. 184.
3. Dean Sherman, *Spiritual Warfare for Every Christian* (Seattle, WA: Frontline Communications, 1990), p. 133.
4. Ibid., p. 150.
5. Quin Sherrer and Ruthanne Garlock, *A Woman's Guide to Spiritual Warfare* (Ann Arbor, MI: Servant Publications, 1991), pp. 84-85.

CHAPTER 7

THE FOURTH MAN IN THE FURNACE

The e-mail message alarmed me. Elijah was in the hospital, and the doctors could not diagnose his illness. With little hope for recovery, death was imminent.

How could this be? I had recently taken a team into Malaysia to minister at the annual church convention for the Latter Rain Church network (this network has no relationship with the Latter Rain Church movement). Elijah's father was not only the founder but also the current president of the organization. The future for this network had seemed so promising. After a long spiritual battle, the churches seemed encouraged and on the verge of pressing forward into God's purposes.

The church network had been through a major split several years prior to this convention. As a result, leaders were discouraged. Churches were only maintaining and not growing. A blanket of death seemed to cover them. Many had lost the vision for their calling. The entire network seemed stuck.

I had been asked to bring a team of ministers to speak at the Latter Rain convention. After arriving, we were able to discern the work of the enemy and sensed the death assignment from Satan. Our teaching, praying and prophesying had been used by the Lord to help break the discouragement and give hope to the churches and leaders. We believed a breakthrough had occurred.

TESTING GOD'S WORD

During the conference, as we ministered to Elijah, the eldest son of the network president and his wife, we became aware of God's call on the young man's life. Elijah was to have a key role in the network. We laid hands on him and released the prophetic word over him. The leadership, as well as the members of the network, agreed with the prophetic words spoken over Elijah.

Shortly after the conference, Elijah began strategizing and making plans for Latter Rain churches. Within two weeks after the end of the conference, Elijah was stricken with the illness. He was taken to a hospital in Malaysia, where the best doctors were available. In spite of the high level of medical expertise, however, Elijah's illness was not diagnosed.

As soon as I received the e-mail prayer alert, I began notifying intercessors around the world. This was a time when we needed the Body of Christ to stand together in prayer. The call of God was that Elijah was to play a key role in the work of the Lord in Malaysia, as well as other nations. The enemy had heard the prophetic word over him and was trying to hinder the fulfillment of that word. The word of the Lord was being tested.

Along with fervent, intense prayer for Elijah, I sent a prayer cloth that had been anointed with oil by my husband, some elders from a church in the United States and me. We also prophesied into a recorder and sent the tape of the prophetic words. The cloth was placed on Elijah's body in Malaysia, and the tape was played continuously in his room in the intensive care unit of the hospital. Within a few days after these prophetic acts, Elijah was healed and dismissed to go home. No diagnosis was ever given for his illness. The word of the Lord had been tested, but Elijah had come through the fiery furnace to do the will of the Father.

Questions flood our minds when situations like that occur. Often we are like the people in Malachi's day, whose belief system reasons that evil people get away with doing wrong and the righteous always seem to suffer.

> You have wearied the LORD with your words. Yet you say, "How have we wearied Him?" In that you say, "Everyone who does evil is good in the sight of the LORD, and He delights in them," or, "Where is the God of justice?" (Mal. 2:17).

In times like these, there are several questions we usually ask:

- Why do good people suffer and sin sometimes seems to go unpunished?
- Isn't God a good and loving God?
- Is suffering and adversity a sign that the suffering person is wicked?

The Bible encourages us to have a spirit of rejoicing when we go through testings and trials. Sometimes it is hard for me to rejoice in the midst of trials. My husband is good at reminding me to do this. He continuously quotes the Scripture found in 1 Thessalonians:

> In everything give thanks; for this is God's will for you in Christ Jesus (5:18).

The Lord is not telling us to thank him *for* the situation but to thank him *in* the situation. We need a spirit of rejoicing to help us overcome in the midst of adversity.

TWO SOURCES OF TESTING

Two different sources of testing are encountered as we seek to fulfill God's call for our lives. The first are tests that come from God. His purpose always is to reveal the gold inside us. This is commonly referred to as the refiner's fire.

> But who can endure the day of His coming? And who can stand when He appears? For He is like a refiner's fire and like fullers' soap. And He will sit as a smelter and purifier of silver, and He will purify the sons of Levi and refine them like gold and silver, so that they may present to the LORD offerings in righteousness (Mal. 3:2-3).

As believers, we are the temple of the Holy Spirit, God's dwelling place. He desires to come and cleanse His holy temple of anything that would defile it. The refining He is doing is bringing us back into the image of Himself. He comes to test our attitudes and motives. He uses these tests to purify us by removing bitterness, selfishness and covetousness. His fire is designed not only to expose our weaknesses but also to cause us to turn to Him for help.

I remember a time when the Lord was taking me through a refiner's fire. I would ask Him to help me break certain habits in my life, which I referred to as weaknesses. One day God spoke a word that got my attention: "Barbara, you need to change the name of the things you are calling weaknesses and habits. If you will call them by the name I call them, then you will be more aggressive in dealing with them. Call them what they are. They are *sin*."

The Lord was right. That word got my attention. The Bible says that when we know to do right and don't do it, it is sin.

> Therefore, to one who knows the right thing to do, and does not do it, to him it is sin (Jas. 4:17).

When I began to see my character flaws the way the Lord saw them, they were easier to deal with and did not take as long to eradicate.

One of the words for "testing" in the Bible is the Greek word *dokimion*.

> Knowing that the *testing* of your faith produces endurance (Jas. 1:3, emphasis added).

Zodhiates says the word "dokimion" is the "means of proving, a criterion, test, by which anything is proved or tried, as faith by afflictions."[1] The Lord uses tests to prove the good, or gold, that is in us. He does not use tests to disapprove or destroy us.

The trials we go through are the means of testing us to bring forth the good. In James 1:2,12-14 we find the word "trial," which is also used as a means of testing.

> Consider it all joy, my brethren, when you encounter various *trials* (Jas. 1:2, emphasis added).

The word "trial" in the Greek language is *peirasmos*. The root word means experience. The meaning of the word "peirasmos" depends on who is doing the testing. If it is God, the trial is for the purpose of proving someone and never for the purpose of causing one to fall. If the testing is from the enemy, the trial is expressly for the purpose of causing one to fall.[2] In James 1:13 we find the word "tempt"; in the Greek language the word is *peirazo*. It is a word that means to tempt or prove by soliciting to sin. The difference between dokimazo (testing) and peirazo (tempted) is that the latter has the intention of proving that one has been evil or to make him evil. The intent of dokimazo is to prove someone good and acceptable. Satan tempts (peirazo) to show someone unapproved. Satan is even called *pierastes*, the tempter.[3] Several examples of the word "peirazo" are in the Bible (Matt. 22:18,35; 1 Thess. 3:5). One example is when the Pharisees and Sadducees were trying to prove Jesus as evil.

> The Pharisees and Sadducees came up, and testing Him asked
> Him to show them a sign from heaven (Matt. 16:1).

The religious leaders constantly tested Jesus to try to entice him to sin or to find evil in Him. None of their testing succeeded. Jesus was without sin and perfect in His ways.

An example of the word "dokimazo" can be found in one of Peter's epistles.

> In this you greatly rejoice, even though now for a little while,
> if necessary, you have been distressed by various trials, that the
> proof of your faith, being more precious than gold which is
> perishable, even though tested by fire, may be found to result
> in praise and glory and honor at the revelation of Jesus Christ
> (1 Pet. 1:6-7).

Is there a contradiction between these words and the following Scripture, found in Genesis?

And it came to pass after these things, that God did tempt

Abraham, and said unto him, Abraham: and he said, Behold, here I am (Gen. 22:1, *KJV*).

At the time of the writing of the *King James Version*, the word "tempt" was translated "to test," rather than the current meaning of "to entice to do wrong." Since God does not tempt us, the translation of the word for tempt over time became a problem. God was not tempting Abraham to sin; rather, he was testing his character.

TESTED IN SEVERAL AREAS

As we pursue the call of God, we will be tested in several areas, one of which is our character. Job had his character tested in an exceptionally severe trial. He was a good man who was devastated in one day. Job lost everything he had, including his 10 children.

Later Job was stricken with a terrible disease. His friends thought he had sinned. Job couldn't understand why all this was happening to him. However, he knew that in time he would be vindicated. Job willingly allowed the test to purify him. As a result of this process, Job received a revelation of God.

I have heard of Thee by the hearing of the ear; but now my eye sees Thee; therefore I retract, and I repent in dust and ashes (Job 42:5-6).

God vindicated Job and then had Job pray for his friends, who encountered the wrath of God. As Job came through the fiery trial, he was *proved* and *approved* by God (see 42:9). His character was tested in the fiery furnace of difficulties. Like Job, we will walk through difficulties. In those times of testing of our character, we can come out with the same results as Job.

But He knows the way I take; when He has tried me, I shall come forth as gold (Job 23:10).

We can come not only into restoration but also into an increase (see 42:10).

Restoration means we will gain more than we lost. Matthew Henry's commentary articulates God's restoration in Job's life. This promise is also for our lives, as we experience difficulty while pursing the call of God.

> God doubled Job's possessions. We may lose much for the Lord, but we shall not lose any thing by him. Whether the Lord gives us health and temporal blessings or not, if we patiently suffer according to his will, in the end we shall be happy. Job's estate increased. The blessing of the Lord makes rich; it is he that gives us power to get wealth, and gives success in honest endeavors. The last days of a good man sometimes prove his best, his last works his best works, his last comforts his best comforts; for his path, like that of the morning light, shines more and more unto the perfect day.[4]

Not only is our character tested as we walk in our call, but our prophetic words are also tested. At age 17 Joseph received a prophetic dream concerning his future. After the dream, he went through years of testing of the word. His prophetic word had to be tested before he could own the promise. God was faithful through those times to bring Joseph into the call on his life.

> Until the time that his word came to pass, the word of the LORD tested him (Ps. 105:19).

Several years ago a couple was expecting their first baby. Prophetic words were spoken over the unborn child concerning his future. Those who prophesied the baby's destiny were trustworthy prophetic people. When the baby was born, he lingered on the threshold of death. The doctors gave the parents no hope that the child would live.

Intercessors were notified of the crisis. The parents and intercessors recalled the prophetic words that had been spoken as a weapon against the enemy of death. For weeks they did not see a change in the baby's condition. However, they were filled with faith and would not give up. They knew the word of the Lord was more powerful than the outward circumstances. After several weeks of intense spiritual battle, the baby's condition took a turn and he was totally healed. The prophetic word had been tested until there was a manifestation of those words.

In the same way that we use the Scriptures, the written Word, as a weapon of warfare, we must also use prophetic words as a weapon. During those times when the word is being tested, we must allow the Lord to fill us with a new level of faith. It takes faith initially to receive the prophetic word. A greater level of faith is required when the word is tested.

Another area that gets tested as we advance is the call of God on our lives. Relatives, both natural and spiritual, may not grasp or approve of our calling. Joseph's brothers were filled with jealousy and envy when he told them about his call (see Gen. 37). Potiphar's wife falsely accused him, and Joseph ended up in prison as an innocent man (see Gen. 39). Government officials had erased him from their minds, but he was not forgotten by God. The Lord gave favor to Joseph, and he eventually was able to fulfill the call of his youthful prophetic dream. The call was tested before it came into fullness.

Over and over again we are tempted to think that God has changed His mind about our call, particularly when we are in the midst of difficulties. Sometimes we think the prophetic word we received was a false prophecy. It is then we must allow the Lord to bring us through the testing of our call. Often He is doing things we cannot see. There is a greater level of anointing and authority waiting for those who come through the fiery furnace of testing.

THE FIERY FURNACE OF TESTING

A picture of the fiery furnace of testing is found in the book of Daniel. Three men with the names of Shadrach, Meshach and Abed-nego were ordered to be thrown into a flaming furnace because they would not worship any god but the true God. King Nebuchadnezzar ordered the furnace to be heated seven times hotter than usual. These three men made a declaration that their God was able to deliver them from the furnace. They also declared that even if He did not, they would not serve any other god.

The three men were bound up and cast into the furnace. Later, as the king looked inside, he saw a sight that caused him to issue a decree against anyone who spoke against the true God.

> Then Nebuchadnezzar the king was astounded and stood up in haste; he responded and said to his high officials, "Was it not three men we cast bound into the midst of the fire?" They replied to the king, "Certainly, O king." He answered and said, "Look! I see four men loosed and walking about in the midst of the fire without harm, and the appearance of the fourth is like a son of the gods" (Dan. 3:24-25).

Even though the king witnessed the three men tied up and cast into the furnace of blazing fire, he then saw them set free and loosed and walking around in the furnace. Miraculously, the three men were not alone in the furnace. A fourth man was walking with them: Jesus was in the furnace with those three men. Shadrach, Meshach and Abed-nego came out from the furnace untouched by the fire and without the smell of smoke on them. The fire had no effect on the bodies of these men, nor was a hair on their heads singed. Then the king caused the three men to prosper in the province of Babylon.

As we walk through the furnace of affliction, Jesus will walk with us. He will only allow the furnace to burn up the things that keep us bound and prevent us from being formed again into His image. We can come forth without the smell of the smoke of bitterness, anger and self-pity. He changes the smell of the furnace to the sweet smell of the incense of a life sacrificed to Him. Only God will be blessed and glorified.

As we walk in the call of God, we will go through the fiery furnace. We will go through the floodwaters. We will encounter the enemy who comes as a roaring lion. Yet the Lord will be with us.

> When you pass through the waters, I will be with you; and through the rivers, they will not overflow you. When you walk

through the fire, you will not be scorched, nor will the flame burn you (Isa. 43:2).

Why do we go through these hard places? As we allow God to take us through them, we become the chosen of the Lord.

Behold, I have refined you, but not as silver; I have tested you in the furnace of affliction (Isa. 48:10).

In this verse the word "tested" is *bachar* in the Hebrew language. "Bachar" means "chosen or selected; selected from the choicest."[5] As we go through the furnace of affliction, the Lord, the fourth man in the furnace, walks with us. He chooses us as selected ones from the choicest on Earth.

Not only are we refined and chosen in the furnace of affliction, but we are also there for another purpose. The Lord releases a greater level of authority in our lives. We go through the furnace to teach the furnace a lesson—that we can go through the fire and not be burned! We go through the waters to teach the waters a lesson—that we will not be drowned! We encounter the roaring lion to teach the lion a lesson—that there is a lion of the tribe of Judah, and He has prevailed (see Rev. 5:5).

THE REAL STORY
OVERCOMING THE FURNACE IN MY LIFE

Testimony by Alice Smith
Executive Director, U.S. Prayer Center, Houston, Texas

My Baptist background closed all outside doors for prophetic words. But when we seek Him with all our heart, God will break through our misconceptions and man-made traditions. Such was the case in June of 1985. My schedule was busy with a new infant and a growing family. Since I was a choir teacher for the children at church, my prayer time began early each morning. But this particular prayer time was different.

As I lay prostrate on the floor, the Lord began to speak to my heart. His was not an unfamiliar voice, for I had developed the ability to hear Him. The Lord spoke gently and clearly, telling me to turn to a Scripture passage. Once I found the text, I broke into tears. These words resonated in my spirit, and I somehow knew they would come to pass.

> I will make an everlasting covenant with you. Surely you will summon nations you know not, and nations that do not know you will hasten to you, because of the LORD your God (see Isa. 55:3-5).

The revelation was given to me that day, but the testing of this word came at a high price. I realized that the Lord was looking for several actions on my part, including:

- It was my job to be still, stay faithful, keep my mouth shut and wait with expectancy for the revelation to come to pass. It took 10 years for the fulfillment. Today, I minister in nations all over the world.
- The Lord allowed many kinds of trials to come to test my faith. This allowed my faith to be strengthened, my soul purified and my intentions checked.

Every prophetic word I have received has been an invitation from the Lord, not a proclamation. Though adverse circumstances may come, the Father monitors our willingness to lose all and gain Him.

DISCUSSION QUESTIONS

1. We need a spirit of _____ when we go through testing and trials.
2. What are the two sources of testing we encounter?
3. What is the purpose of God's refining fire?
4. What is the purpose of the tests the enemy brings?

5. Explain the reference in Genesis 22:1 where "God tested Abraham."

6. What are three areas in our lives that get tested?

7. Restoration means we _____ more than we _____.

8. Describe times when your character, your prophetic word (or promise from the Lord) and your call were tested.

9. What is burned in the furnace of affliction?

10. Where are we chosen?

11. What is released to us in the fiery furnace?

12. Who is in the furnace with us?

Notes

1. Spiros Zodhiates, *The Hebrew Greek Key Study Bible, New American Standard, Lexical Aids to the New Testament* (La Habra, CA: AMG Publishers, 1990), p. 1826.

2. Ibid., p. 1866.

3. Ibid.

4. Logos Library System, *Matthew Henry's Concise Commentary on the Bible* (La Habra, CA: Lockman Foundation, 1998), n.p.

5. Logos Library System, *New American Standard Bible Greek Dictionary*, updated ed. (La Habra, CA: Lockman Foundation, 1995), p. 977.

CHAPTER 8

RECEIVING A NEW IDENTITY

Throughout the weekend, Dale and I kept reminding our children to use as little water as possible. "Take quick showers," we told them. "Don't leave water running any longer than absolutely necessary." This was because on Friday morning the water had been backing up into our tubs, showers and toilets. After calling the plumber, we were told it would be Monday before a serviceman could check out the problem. Meanwhile, we had to be very careful not to allow much water to go down our drains.

On Monday, after evaluating our situation, the serviceman called for me to come to our front yard. "I want you to see what the problem is," he said. I followed him to a large hole he had dug in our yard. "I like to dig a big hole," he explained. "I want to be able to get a good look at what is going on."

While I looked into the hole, he made clear to me what had caused the problem with our water drains. "The large trees in your yard developed a root system. These roots totally clogged up your pipes. Therefore, no water can get through. I will have to remove the roots to clear out the pipes. Not only that," he went on, "but someone was here before and attempted to repair this situation. There is a broken pipe in the ground. Rather than repairing the pipe, they simply covered it up, so the broken place was out of sight."

After a few hours of work, the repairman asked me to turn on the dishwasher and every faucet in the house and to flush all the toilets. To my delight the water flowed through the pipes without delay. All the obstruction was removed. The pipes could now do what they were designed to do. Roots had been removed, and broken places were mended.

MAKING STRAIGHT THE PATH FOR THE FREE FLOW OF GOD'S SPIRIT

As I stood there, rejoicing in the results of the completed work, the Holy Spirit spoke to my heart. "This is what I want to do in my people. Hidden roots prevent them from being able to do what they are designed to do. Broken places have been covered up. The water of My Spirit cannot flow through them freely. I want to remove the bad roots and give them new roots. I desire to mend the broken places in their lives, so they come into wholeness. Then I will be able to pour My Spirit through them in a powerful way."

The primary function of roots is to hold a plant in place and supply it with nourishment from the soil. It is a part of plants that is necessary for growth. Likewise, roots are found in the hearts of mankind. These roots have been planted through deep hurts, wounds, fears and/or a life of sin. Because the soil of the heart has not been cleansed and healed, the roots have grown.

Several years ago we cut down a tree in our backyard. For the next few years, new growth continued to sprout from the place where the tree had been. We kept cutting down the growth only to see it sprout up again within a short period of time. What was the problem? Although the visible growth of the tree had been cut down, the root system was still intact. Because roots are still alive, they keep producing life. Jesus taught about fruit in the Bible. He said a good tree bears good fruit and a bad tree bears bad fruit. Trees that do not bear good fruit are to be cut down. He also said that grapes are not gathered from thorn bushes, nor are figs gathered from thistles.

So then, you will know them by their fruits (Matt. 7:20).

Bad fruit comes from a bad root. If there is a good root, it will produce good fruit.

Bad roots may go back to any period during life. Often they involve a hurt or wounding from a close relationship. They can also be a result of sin or occultic involvement. When a person overreacts to a situation, it shows an area that needs healing. Sometimes it may be a demonic influence, but many times it is simply a manifestation of a hurt soul.

A person does not need to dig for the root through introspection, as introspection is part of the problem. Looking at self will only make matters worse. The Holy Spirit searches our hearts and shows us areas that need forgiveness applied.

> I, the LORD, search the heart, I test the mind (Jer. 17:10).

We need to forgive people and circumstances when the Spirit of God reveals the need for forgiveness, for it is the "root out of parched ground" (Isa. 53:1)—Jesus, the root of Jesse—who made provision for us to be set free.

> Surely our griefs He Himself bore, and our sorrows He carried; yet we ourselves esteemed Him stricken, smitten of God, and afflicted. But He was pierced through for our transgressions, He was crushed for our iniquities; the chastening for our well-being fell upon Him, and by His scourging we are healed (Isa. 53:4-5).

As the axe is laid to the root, healing and deliverance come to the captives. The Lord is then able to freely pour the water of His Spirit through those vessels.

RESTORING WHAT WAS LOST

Someone once said, "We are born remembering what we lost." I spoke of mankind being created to be the image bearers of the Lord (see chapter 5.) Man was to walk in God's authority and have dominion in the earth. He was to be a reflection of the Lord. Due to the Fall and evil in the earth, man lost his identity as God's image bearer. As a fallen creature, he lost the authority and dominion as God's representative in the earth. However, Jesus came to bring healing and restoration to His people. He came to do more than cause us to *remember* what we lost. He came to *restore* all that was lost.

When Adam and Eve sinned, they immediately ran from the presence of the Lord.

> They heard the sound of the LORD God walking in the garden
> in the cool of the day, and the man and his wife hid themselves
> from the presence of the LORD God among the trees of the
> garden (Gen. 3:8).

Looking at themselves, Adam and Eve realized their condition of nakedness. In order to hide their condition, they made themselves coverings of fig leaves. Since that time, mankind has been attempting to cover himself with false images and running from the presence of the Lord. The only path for restoration is to allow the Holy Spirit to reveal and release the false identity. We must run into the presence of the Lord and cease running from Him.

As a result of Adam and Eve's fall in the garden, their eyes were opened to the natural world and closed to the godly spiritual world. They looked away from God and started to study self (see v. 7). The study of self is a form of idolatry. Man, in looking at self, had become self-conscious rather than God-conscious. We become like what we worship (see chapter 4). Man, therefore, began to worship self—the creature, rather than the creator (see Rom. 1:18-32). As a result, man began to find his identity in self, rather than in God. The process of restoration can only occur when man reverses his attention from self and once again looks at God. To receive a new identity, we must see through the eyes of faith and not merely look through natural eyes.

Moses looked through the eyes of faith and was able to fulfill his call from God.

> [Motivated] by faith he left Egypt behind him, being unawed
> and undismayed by the wrath of the king; for he never flinched
> but held staunchly to his purpose and endured steadfastly as
> one who gazed on Him Who is invisible (Heb. 11:27, *AMP*).

The Scripture is not speaking of Israel's exodus from Egypt but of Moses' leaving Egypt after killing the Egyptian. Moses realized his identity was not that of an Egyptian. He was an Israelite. When he came into the revelation of who he was created to be, he renounced his old life in the palace. His decision indicated he realized he was meant to share life with his own people. Because of his decision to walk in a new identity, he became stalwart against the king's wrath.

Moses was able to walk in great courage because he saw an invisible monarch greater than Pharaoh. During the 40 years spent in Midian, Moses lived for his great destiny. He trusted God in spite of his decision to flee Egypt. Chapter 11 of Hebrews tells us that he "endured steadfastly." The word "endured" in Greek is *kartereo*. It means Moses endured severe yet voluntary exile with strength and courage.[1] He was able to remain steadfast, knowing his call, because he gazed on Him who is invisible. This type of faith produces miracles and restores lost identity.

RECOGNIZING THE BATTLEGROUND FOR RESTORATION

The battleground for restoration of true identity is in our minds. The Bible says that when man failed to worship God, his mind was filled with wrong thinking.

> Because when they knew and recognized Him as God, they did not honor and glorify Him as God or give Him thanks. But instead they became futile and godless in their thinking [with vain imaginings, foolish reasoning, and stupid speculations] and their senseless minds were darkened (Rom. 1:21, *AMP*).

Man became dull and sluggish in his imaginations. Idolatry is the practice of the presence of evil; it is not merely bowing down to carved images. Idolatry is the bowing down to whatever image exalts itself against God.

Restoration involves looking away from the idol of self and looking at the presence of God. Isaiah, the prophet, said that looking on the face of idols starved the people's imaginations. Isaiah exhorted the people to look away from those idols and look instead toward the creator.

Lift up your eyes on high, and see who has created these stars (Isa. 40:26).

Oswald Chambers speaks of God restoring the starved imagination in his book *My Utmost for His Highest*:

> The test of spiritual concentration is bringing the imagination into captivity. Is your imagination looking on the face of an idol? Is the idol yourself? Your work? Your conception of what a worker should be? Your experience of salvation and sanctification? Then your imagination of God is starved, and when you are up against difficulties you have no power, you can only endure in darkness. If your imagination is starved, do not look back to your own experience; it is God Whom you need. Go right out of yourself, away from the face of your idols, away from everything that has been starving your imagination. Rouse yourself, take the gibe that Isaiah gave the people, and deliberately turn your imagination to God.[2]

Knowledge itself cannot redeem us. That is an occultic concept which teaches that we learn about truth, and truth gives salvation. Jesus said,

> And you shall know the truth, and the truth shall make you free (John 8:32).

The word "know" in Greek is *ginosko*. It means "to come to know, recognize, or perceive."[3] Ginosko is not the accumulation of knowledge. The word carries with it the connotation of intimate communion between you and a person you know to be truth.

> Fixing our eyes on Jesus, the author and perfecter of faith (Heb. 12:2).

Our minds must be fixed on Jesus, rather than on the hurts, wounds, fears, inadequacies and failures of self, or the sinful deeds of another person.

For those who are according to the flesh set their minds on the things of the flesh, but those who are according to the Spirit, the things of the Spirit (Rom. 8:5).

Those who are "[in] the flesh" are people who habitually allow their minds to dwell on things that continually well up within the sinful nature. Their minds are set on sinful practices of self or others.

To be spiritually minded is to have a mind possessed by the Spirit. As believers, the Lord has called us to be spiritually minded. We are to yield to the life of God within us. As His life is allowed to arise, it will bring us into peace. One of the meanings of "peace" is *phimoo*, "to muzzle."[4] The life of God within is able to muzzle the voices of the flesh and the enemy. We hear His voice, and His voice breaks the power of all the other negative voices that have spoken to us.

HEALING THROUGH LISTENING TO GOD

Listening to the Lord is one of the most vital things we can do for healing to occur. He will send a word that dismantles the negative voices of the past. Leanne Payne discusses the necessity of listening prayer in her book *The Broken Image*:

> The fallen self cannot know itself. . . . We do not know who we are and will search for our identity in someone or something other than God until we find ourselves in Him. And it is only in Him that we become persons. In the Presence, conversing with Him, we find that the "old man"—the sinful, the neurotic, the sickly compulsive, the seedy old actor within—is not *the Real*, but that these are simply the false selves that can never be rooted in God. We find that God is the Real and that He calls the real "I" forward, separating us from our sicknesses and sins. We then no longer define ourselves by our sins, neuroses, and deprivations, but by Him whose healing life cleanses and indwells us. . . . We find that we are in Him and that He is in us.

Thus in His Presence, listening to the word the Spirit sends, spiritual and psychological healing takes place. Our Lord sends a word—of joy, judgment, instruction, guidance. And that word, if hidden away in an obedient heart, will work toward integration of that personality. As I listen and obey, I *become*.[5]

HEALING THROUGH FORGIVENESS

Forgiveness is vital if we are to come into healing and have a new identity released. That is why it is so important to ask the Lord to search our heart and reveal those who need to be forgiven. Sometimes we forgive as an act of our will and not because we feel like forgiving. We do so out of obedience because Jesus said we should. We forgive in order to be forgiven.

Whenever you stand praying, forgive, if you have anything against anyone; so that your Father also who is in heaven may forgive you your transgressions. [But if you do not forgive, neither will your Father who is in heaven forgive your transgressions] (Mark 11:25-26).

When we don't forgive, we will be controlled to a certain extent by the person we refuse to forgive. It seems as though we cannot go anywhere without encountering that person. Our thoughts are captured by what the person did. When we forgive, we take away the other person's weapons against us. The Lord is then able to pour His healing love into us. He can be to us what the other person was not able to be.

SEEKING THE PROCESS OF WHOLENESS

Wholeness does not come instantly; it is a process. Although there are times of instantaneous healing encounters with the Lord, a discipline is required to come into wholeness. Learning to recognize that the

Lord is with us and in us at all times requires a concerted effort of the will. I remember asking the Lord to teach me what it is to pray at all times (see Eph. 6:18).

- Must I always speak in an audible voice?
- How does this kind of praying fit in with times of sleep?
- Will I be able to concentrate on other activities if I am always praying?

It took a while for me to understand what praying at all times actually means. God desired that I would continually be so aware of His presence that I would realize I was never separated from Him. I came to know that He is not limited to a certain place or a certain day of the week. As I developed a sense of His omnipresence, it became easier to talk with Him, hear His voice and receive His strength. I then could begin to see with the eyes of faith. His promise is that He is always with us (see Matt. 28:20).

RECEIVING A NEW NAME

As we consciously abide in the Lord, He speaks a word and gives us a new name. Frequently we have names that have identified us from the past. Some of our names may be Failure, Rejected, Abandoned, Ugly, Inadequate or Abused. Jesus will speak a new name that will break the power of the old name that life and circumstances have given us. The new name the Lord speaks sets us on a new path to success.

The nations will see your righteousness, and all kings your glory; and you will be called by a new name, which the mouth of the LORD will designate. You will also be a crown of beauty in the hand of the LORD, and a royal diadem in the hand of your God. It will no longer be said to you, "Forsaken," nor to your land will it any longer be said, "Desolate"; but you will be called, "My delight is in her," and your land, "Married"; for the

LORD delights in you, and to Him your land will be married (Isa. 62:2-4).

God the Father delights to name His children. His fathering Spirit reveals our true identity. He revealed the Father's heart at the Jordan when Jesus was baptized.

And behold, [there was] a voice out of the heavens saying, "This is My beloved Son, in whom I am well-pleased" (Matt. 3:17).

It has been said, "A man is not a man until his father tells him he is a man." We yearn for the affirmation of who we truly are apart from our parents and close relationships. When these people have been unable or unwilling to affirm us, we are not without hope. The Lord is able to speak a healing word and affirm our identity. As we learn to listen for Him to tell us who we really are, the new name brings us out of captivity and establishes us in a new place.

Joshua had been a warrior under the leadership of Moses. As Joshua approached the time for a new season in his life, he needed a new identity. He would no longer be just one of the warriors. No longer would he be able to depend on Moses to make the critical decisions for the nation of Israel. He would now be the leader to take a nation into its destiny. Joshua needed a new name to empower him to fulfill his call for the new season. Moses, as a spiritual father, changed Joshua's name.

But Moses called Hoshea the son of Nun, Joshua (Num. 13:16).

MAINTAINING OUR NEW IDENTITY

A process must be walked out in order to maintain our new identity. Standing in faith is crucial. We are born again by faith. Therefore, we must receive by faith, not by feelings, the work the Lord has accomplished in our lives. Feelings do not always tell the truth.

We must first recognize that old feelings are simply powerless ghosts from the past, and we cannot give life to them by agreeing with them.

O Lord, our God, other masters besides You have ruled over us, but we will acknowledge and mention Your name only. They [the former tyrant masters] are dead, they shall not live and reappear; they are powerless ghosts, they shall not rise and come back. Therefore You have visited and made an end of them and caused every memory of them [every trace of their supremacy] to perish (Isa. 26:13-14, *AMP*).

Next, we must acknowledge the presence of the Lord. Satan has won no victories in my life. Jesus has taken every hurtful thing and turned it into nourishment to cause me to grow into the person He created me to be. The enemy may have tried to bring defeat, but he lost every battle. Jesus won them all!

Finally, we must learn to laugh at our mistakes. I remember a very difficult time in my life when I thought there was no hope for a brighter day. As I basked in the presence of the Lord, I clearly heard Him say, "Barbara, I am bigger than your mistakes." What a revelation! Even though theologically I could explain this revelation, my deep heart had not known it to be truth. Yet when the Lord spoke His healing word, I was changed on the inside. I started laughing, as a new joy filled me at that moment. Rather than allowing the circumstances to devastate me, I could now laugh at my own mistakes. Father God was more powerful than any mistakes I could make. He is able to fix anything I did wrong and uses it for my good. Isn't He amazing? Aren't you glad He is holding on to us much harder than we are holding on to Him? Have you laughed at your mistakes recently? If not, do so. You deserve a joy break today!

THE REAL STORY
RECEIVING A NEW IDENTITY IN MY LIFE

Testimony by Barbara J. Yoder
Michigan State Coordinator, Strategic Prayer Network
Cofounder and Senior Pastor, Shekinah Christian Church,
Ann Arbor, Michigan

I grew up as the middle child in a family of five. I was always being compared with my older sister, who was successful academically and graduated as salutatorian in high school. Teachers constantly told me I was not achieving and asked me why I was not like my sister. They were probably trying to encourage me to reach my potential, but all I heard was that I was dumb, stupid and unable to achieve.

Through a process of coming into a personal relationship with God, I discovered that He personally designed me to fulfill a unique destiny. Furthermore, I realized that He had placed within my spiritual DNA the ability to succeed. So I began to develop confidence. As a result, I began to work hard, became a straight-A student and was granted a full tuition and housing fellowship. However, my progress took my believing what God said about me and then behaving accordingly. I remember having to read the Bible out loud to myself as a declaration of who God was and who He said I was. Through that process I heard the Word. That hearing produced faith in my heart to believe God had given me a new identity.

DISCUSSION QUESTIONS

1. How are bad roots planted in people's hearts?
2. How did Adam and Eve react to God's presence after they sinned?
3. The study of self is a form of _____.
4. Where is the battleground for restoration of our true identity?

5. What were the people of Isaiah's day looking at? What happened to them?
6. Explain the Hindu concept for salvation, as well as the Christian concept.
7. What does the mind of the flesh dwell on?
8. What does the spiritually minded person's mind dwell on?
9. What are the two most vital things we can do for healing to occur?
10. Ask the Lord to tell you your old name.
11. Ask Him to speak the new name He has given you. What is your real name?
12. Have you laughed at yourself today?

Notes

1. Spiros Zodhiates, *The Hebrew Greek Key Study Bible, New American Standard, Lexical Aids to the New Testament* (La Habra, CA: AMG Publishers, 1990), p. 1845.
2. Oswald Chambers, *My Utmost for His Highest* (New York: Dodd, Mead and Company, 1935), p. 41.
3. Logos Library System, *New American Standard Bible Greek Dictionary*, updated version (La Habra, CA: Lockman Foundation, 1995), p. 1097.
4. W. E. Vine, *Vine's Expository Dictionary of New Testament Words* (McLean, VA: MacDonald Publishing Company, n.d.), p. 853.
5. Leanne Payne, *The Broken Image* (Westchester, IL: Crossway Books, 1981), pp. 149-50.

CHAPTER 9

RELATIONSHIPS FOR DESTINY

Tears welled up in the pastor's eyes as he told the story of his loneliness. He had been pastoring in this southwestern town for about four years, yet his attempts to reach out to other pastors had failed. The church he pastored had been through many hurts before he arrived. Therefore, people didn't trust one another, and they didn't trust leadership. The struggle for loving relationships had been long and difficult.

Out of desperation for fellowship, the pastor had recently joined Alcoholics Anonymous. He did not drink and had never been an alcoholic, yet he knew the reputation of the organization. The pastor realized he could find people who would listen to him and care about him. Although he knew God loved him and cared for him, he still needed people who cared. He needed the support of friendship during a difficult time in his life.

KNOWING IT IS NOT GOOD FOR MAN TO BE ALONE

I was amazed at his story. How could a person who loved God and had a call on his life reach a place of not being able to find a true friend? I am afraid that this pastor is not alone in his lack of meaningful relationships. Not everyone will be so desperate for friendships that they join a group like Alcoholics Anonymous, but they go to many other extremes. Some are so desperate that they become suicidal or fall into various forms of sin.

God knew from the beginning that man needed meaningful relationships in his life. With each part God created, He would judge His creation and pronounce, "It is good." The only thing God did not judge as good in creation was the "aloneness" of man.

> Then the LORD God said, "It is not good for the man to be alone;
> I will make him a helper suitable for him" (Gen. 2:18).

God is a relational God. Before the creation of mankind, God had a relationship with His Son. Jesus referred to God as "Father." Fatherhood always implies relationship. Children are an extension of the relationship of the father and mother. Our activities should be an outward expression of our heart relationship to God. How we relate to God should also be reflected in our relationships with others. When we are secure in our relationship with our heavenly Father, meaningful relationships will develop with other people.

I have come across ministers who were in the ministry to meet their own psychological needs. Because of a need for acceptance, the ministry has met that need. Although ministry includes times of rejection, we will always find those who love and accept us.

Ministry should never be attempted to meet personal needs for acceptance. God's call emanates from a loving relationship with Him and a love for people. Ministry is to be a place of loving both God and people so much that we are willing to give our life away. The primary purpose is not receiving, even though we will receive as we give out. Father God demonstrated this principle of giving when He sent His Son to redeem us.

> For God so loved the world, that He gave His only begotten
> Son, that whoever believes in Him should not perish, but have
> eternal life (John 3:16).

REALIZING NOT ALL
RELATIONSHIPS ARE GOOD

God has purposed for our lives to be filled with good relationships. However, not all relationships are good. Some can even be detrimental. Relationships that require constant maintenance can deplete our energy and keep us from being productive. When we have to work constantly at the relationship and spend much time working through disagreements, we are unable to focus on anything else. We find ourselves in a web that entangles us and squeezes the life out of us.

I remember a time when we opened our home to a needy young Christian lady. She had a history of rejection and abandonment. In our naiveté we brought her into our home to try to show her what normal family relationships are to be like. From the day she entered our home, there was constant turmoil. Our normally peaceful, loving, happy home became a battlefield. Our children were unable to sleep at night. Life became drudgery, as we struggled to get through the day without a major war. Prayer and personal ministry were provided for the young lady, yet nothing seemed to work.

After a lengthy period of time, we asked her to leave. That was when a major war broke out. This lady came up with an almost unlimited number of schemes in an attempt to stay. Friends hundreds of miles away were told lies about us. She seemingly had the ability to outwit even the brightest people. After a long tug at our minds and hearts, we had to get the police to remove her from our home.

We realized then that not every relationship is from God, and not every relationship will work. Too often, as Christians, we are of the opinion that we should be friends with everyone. Some people, however, are not looking for friendship. Rather, they are looking for someone who will allow them to continue in their selfish, sickly ways. Relationships can propel us into our destiny, or they can keep us from it. Some relationships are poisonous. We must be able to discern these poisonous relationships.

Jesus did not develop close relationships with everyone. He was able to discern the hearts of men. He knew the ones who were capable of developing meaningful relationships with Him, and those who were not. We must have the same discernment.

LIVING IN COVENANT RELATIONSHIPS

Family relationships are worth the battle, however. The Lord made families, and we must do everything possible to care for those relationships. Forgiveness and openness in communication can pave the way for healing and restoration within a family. God purposed for the family to live in a covenant relationship.

The family is designed by God to be a visible representation of His family on Earth. The Church is another picture of God's family. How sad that many families and churches are dysfunctional in their relationships. Relationships within the home, the spiritual family and the Church have collapsed. God's intention is for man and woman to be faithful to one another in marriage, yet marriage covenants have been violated. Marriage cannot be based on feelings; it must be based on commitment to the relationship. To be successful in our relationship to God, we must be faithful in our marriage relationship.

The Lord's plan is that His covenant be extended from marriage through the generations. Parents are to nurture and raise up godly children. God's covenant was to be taught to the succeeding generations in order that His blessings could be released in the earth. Parents are instructed to teach God's covenant to their children.

> These words, which I am commanding you today, shall be on your heart; and you shall teach them diligently to your sons and shall talk of them when you sit in your house and when you walk by the way and when you lie down and when you rise up (Deut. 6:6-7).

Keith Intrater discusses the importance of godly offspring.

> God's stated purpose in marriage is to bring about godly off-spring (Mal. 2:15). The production of children who will follow in the footsteps of the covenant is immensely important. Most people underestimate the vital reasons for producing godly offspring. Biblical covenants depend on transgenerational commitment. Biblical covenants demand a link by which God can transfer His covenant to the succeeding generation (Gen. 17:7). Men live one generation at a time, but God lives over the span of many generations. If God is to have a covenant with mankind, He must make that covenant span more than one generation. A single generation covenant falls short of a rela-

tionship with God because He is eternal. All of God's covenants with mankind must have a provision for carrying that covenant to unlimited generations in the future.[1]

The relationship of friendship is different from a covenant relationship. Jesus is closer to us than a relationship of friendship.

There is a friend who sticks closer than a brother (Prov. 18:24).

When we become members of the family of God, the Lord is a covenant friend who will stick closer to us than a brother who is in our natural family. The Lord is a faithful covenant friend.

Jonathan and David were covenant friends. They were faithful to one another in good times and difficult times. Their level of commitment went deeper than natural family ties. Jonathan gave up his own destiny for the throne so that David might come into God's destiny for his life. Jonathan's level of faithfulness was a place of dying to self.

Greater love has no one than this, that one lay down his life for his friends (John 15:13).

DEVELOPING TRUST IN RELATIONSHIPS

Paul told Timothy to find faithful men, who would in turn commit to other faithful men and invest Paul's life in them.

The things which you have heard from me in the presence of many witnesses, these entrust to faithful men, who will be able to teach others also (2 Tim. 2:2).

As mentioned earlier, Jesus did not commit Himself to all men but was discerning in His relationships.

But Jesus, on His part, was not entrusting Himself to them, for He knew all men, and because He did not need anyone to bear witness concerning man for He Himself knew what was in man (John 2:24-25).

Jesus knew some men were untrustworthy. Therefore, He chose men who had the potential of being trusted. Jesus spent time with these men until they came to the place where He could deposit trust in them. Often, as believers we think we are to trust everyone. Jesus didn't, and neither should we. Trust must be earned. It is possible to love someone without trusting them.

By the time our children were age 12, they each wanted to drive the car. I tried to explain all the reasons they were not allowed to do this. No matter how I explained it, they still could not understand. Finally, I told them I loved them with my whole heart, but I did not trust them for one moment behind the wheel of the car. They had never been through driver's education. It was illegal to drive at their age. They had no experience in driving. My lack of trust in their driving ability had nothing to do with love. While I loved them dearly, I did not trust them to do something where trust had not been developed.

After a person has been trusted and the trust is broken, restoration is easier said than done. We must allow time for trust to be developed once again. We can and should forgive the person, but it may not be time to trust again. Forgiveness is the first step in restoring trust. By forgiving, we are not saying that what the person did was right. We are simply releasing that person from their debt. Jesus, in teaching His disciples to pray, gave instructions that we must do this, so our own debts are forgiven.

> For if you forgive people their trespasses [their reckless and willful sins, leaving them, letting them go, and giving up resentment], your heavenly Father will also forgive you. But if you do not forgive others their trespasses [their reckless and willful sins, leaving them, letting them go, and giving up resentment], neither will your Father forgive you your trespasses (Matt. 6:14-15, *AMP*).

We forgive, not knowing what the person's reaction to our forgiveness will be. Often, we forgive and hope the person will be as loving and accepting as we want them to be. At times, however, this simply does not happen. Not everyone is trustworthy, but we should forgive anyway. Our forgiveness releases the person into the hands of the Lord. Forgiveness opens the door for God's restoration and healing in our own lives as well as the person who was untrustworthy.

The next thing to do in rebuilding trust is to trust the person in some small matter. If he or she proves faithful in that, then the amount of trust can gradually be increased.

> His master said to him, Well done, you upright (honorable, admirable) and faithful servant! You have been faithful and trustworthy over a little; I will put you in charge of much. Enter into and share the joy (the delight, the blessedness) which your master enjoys (Matt. 25:23, *AMP*).

Many times after forgiving a person, we want to rush in and trust the person for something big before they have proven they are trustworthy.

A trustworthy friend should be able to hold confidences. If the person is unable to hold confidential information, he will be unable to hold a covenant relationship. We should reveal only a small amount of information during the restoring process. Is the person a gossip? Spreading gossip will do more than destroy our friendship with that person; it will destroy our relationship with others. A gossiping tongue is like a cancer that continues to grow. We must be sure we can trust the person to keep confidential small amounts of intimate information before revealing more serious matters.

Finally, we must forgive ourselves. We cannot allow guilt and condemnation to torment us. We are in a learning process. We have not failed; we are simply growing in our call.

EMBRACING THE RESPONSIBILITIES OF COVENANT

Several years ago I was ministering with a team in Malaysia. Covenant relationships were being taught during the church conference. At the end of the meetings the pastor sponsoring the conference spoke to me. "I didn't know anyone believed in covenant today. I certainly didn't know people from America believed in covenant." How surprised I was at his comment. Why would he believe that? Then I realized what he was saying. In today's society people do not understand covenant. Oftentimes, even the people who do understand covenant are not willing to walk in the depth of this approach in relationships.

We live in a disposable society. Things that used to be permanent are now the throwaway variety. We throw away disposable dishes; we throw away clothes that sometimes only need mending; we throw away excess food. We even throw away people because we are a disposable society that throws away relationships. I am not talking about friendships that are designed to destroy us. I am talking about meaningful relationships that God has purposed for our lives. These relationships have been forged in covenant and planned by God to move us into our destiny.

What then is covenant? A covenant is an agreement made between two or more parties in relationship with one another. A covenant is not to be taken lightly. Covenants are not made with just anyone. Covenant relationships have responsibilities. There are also blessings for obedience and curses for disobedience within covenant relationships. For eternity, God is the One who offers covenant with us. He is a covenant-making, covenant-keeping God, and His dealings in the earth are done through His covenant partners.

When our family moved to East Texas many years ago, we needed a new lawn mower. After locating the one we felt would be perfect for us, we went to the service counter to pay for it.

"You don't need to pay the entire amount today," the man volunteered. "You can pay the remaining amount over the next three months. There will be no interest on the amount you owe."

"Great!" my husband exclaimed. "Where is the contract I need to sign?"

"You don't need to sign a contract," the manager offered. "I trust you to pay the amount you owe."

Never had we heard anything like this when making a purchase. The man believed we would keep our promise to him. I am not sure that is a good policy for a businessman nowadays, but it is the way it *should* be. We should be people who will keep our promises to one another. The sad thing is, most people do not. Therefore, we must have written contracts to legally bind us to our word.

Each time we purchase a house, the stack of papers we sign gets thicker. The reason for this is that people do not keep their word. The lending institutions and builders must cover every possibility that man will not do what he has promised. They continue to find areas where buyers have broken their promises, so they create new forms to be signed to guarantee the promises made. God intended for His people to walk in covenant relationships so that each partner in the relationship could trust the word or the promise of the other.

Covenant relationships are vital for accountability. There have been times in my life when I did not see clearly the path I was taking. That is when I needed someone in my life that I could trust to love me enough to tell me the truth. Too often I have seen individuals who said they were walking in a covenant relationship until the other party told them something they did not want to hear—and that was the end of the relationship.

Dr. Kingsley Fletcher speaks about this in his book *The Power of Covenant*:

> Covenant relationships include a built-in level of personal accountability because we relate to one another with a disarming honesty that strips away facades and falsehood. In a true covenant environment, we feel free to admit our failures and recurring challenges in life because we know we won't be rejected for our honesty. Then our covenant partners feel free to speak the truth in love to help us overcome our failures while walking with us through the difficulties. This is covenant living in Christ at its best.[2]

Jesus is the model we follow in our relationships. He gathered those around Him who were able to partner with Him to fulfill His destiny here on Earth. When He went to be with the Father, He left an expression of Himself in the earth. As you and I walk together in loving, meaningful, covenant relationships, we portray the Body of Christ in the earth. It is not about my call and me; it is about the Lord and His purposes. Through walking in covenant relationships, we become part of the Corporate Man, the Body of Christ, in the earth.

THE REAL STORY
RELATIONSHIP FOR MY DESTINY

Testimony by Rev. Jim Hodges
Founder and Director, Federation of Ministers and Churches
Dallas, Texas

A great stirring was taking place in the local Baptist church. A team of evangelists had come from Texas to lead the church in special spiritual awakening services. During those two weeks in 1959, over 20 youth answered the call to full-time church vocational ministry. I was one who answered the call. Daniel Light, another young man, did also.

Most of the young people went to college out of state to prepare for the ministry. I went to college in my home state of West Virginia. Danny went to another college in West Virginia. He walked up to me after those two weeks of meetings and said, "We need to encourage each other in our calling."

After that time, Danny and I would meet on weekends and go minister together in youth retreats and country churches. He would lead the singing/worship one night, and I would bring the message from God's Word. The next night we reversed roles.

Soon it became evident that our friendship was a vehicle to propel both of us into our destinies to become preachers of the gospel. We encouraged and critiqued each other. We held each other accountable in practical things like finances and being responsible in our ministry assignments. We challenged each other in the areas of prayer and study of the Bible.

Without this relationship, which was formed during the early stages of my development, I do not believe I would have fulfilled my destiny in God.

DISCUSSION QUESTIONS

1. Should Christians attempt to have a good relationship with everyone? Why or why not?
2. Name two things that can pave the way for healing and restoration in a family.
3. Why is success in a marriage relationship important?
4. Explain the reason God desires godly offspring.
5. Why should we not trust everyone?
6. Should we trust a person after we have forgiven them? Why?
7. After trust has been broken, why should a person initially be trusted only in small matters?
8. Why is it important to forgive yourself?
9. What is covenant?
10. Why do we need covenant relationships?
11. Describe a time in your life when trust was broken. Would you handle the situation differently today from how you did then? If so, why?
12. Have you forgiven yourself?

Notes

1. Keith Intrater, *Covenant Relationships* (Shippensburg, PA: Destiny Image Publishers, 1989), p. 179.
2. Kingsley Fletcher, *The Power of Covenant* (Ventura, CA: Regal Books, 2000), p. 48.

CHAPTER 10

OVERCOMING JEZEBEL AND CONTROLLING SPIRITS

Joanne sobbed as she told her story. She was a 49-year-old woman, married and the mother of three adult children. Joanne's own mother was now an elderly woman in her 70s and lived about 1,500 miles away on the East Coast. Although the mother lived a great distance away, Joanne felt obligated to call her each day. She could not remember one day in her entire life that she had not talked to her mother—even on her honeymoon.

Memories of a life controlled by her mother tormented Joanne's mind. She felt she was at a breaking point in her life; yet she did not know what to do, particularly since she was a Christian. For that reason, the following questions hampered her response:

- *Aren't Christians supposed to love and honor their parents?*
- *The Bible says we are to submit to those in authority over us. Doesn't this include our parents?*
- *Is it wrong to want to live your own life when you are an adult?*
- *Am I being rebellious because I don't want to call my mother each day?*

· *No matter what I do, I can't seem to please my mother. What am I doing wrong?*

CONTROLLING AND BEING CONTROLLED

Many believers struggle with similar questions and frustrations. Often they have the same history of a significant person in their life who has controlled them. These people either find they are captive to a continuous stream of controllers, or they themselves end up controlling others. Jesus came to set the captives free (see Luke 4:18). For people to be able to advance in the callings of God, they must be free of the controlling spirits seeking to hinder those callings. They also must be free of any attempt on their own part to control others. In other words, we must deal with the issue of control if we are to be successful in our call.

What causes a controlling spirit to operate in someone's life? There are a number of causes, or reasons. One reason people become controllers is that someone tried to control them in the past and, in the process, hurt them. Often those who have been abused become controllers. The person who abused them physically, verbally or sexually gained control over their life. The abused person then made an inner vow: "I will never be controlled again." From that point on, the person makes every effort to remain in control of every possible situation, hoping to avoid any further abuse.

A controlling person may also have grown up under someone else's constant control. Not understanding the reason for the control, the controlled person judged the parent or the caretaker and vowed, "I will never be like that." Unfortunately, these same people find themselves doing the exact thing they said they would never do—controlling or being controlled.

Another reason people become controllers is that they simply don't want to take responsibility for their lives. The controllers prefer others to serve them, while they act in a lazy, irresponsible manner. These people need a host of others around them to do for them what they don't want to do themselves. They simply want to use others for their own selfish purposes.

DISCERNING THE DIFFERENCE BETWEEN GOOD AND BAD CONTROL

Control is not wrong, in and of itself. The abuse caused by control, however, is definitely wrong. In fact, the Bible teaches us to have *good* control in our lives.

- We are to be led or controlled by the Spirit of God (see Rom. 8:14).
- We should control our tongues (see 1 Pet. 3:10).
- A fruit of the spirit is self-control (see Gal. 5:22-23).

Controlling boundaries are a means of protection from irresponsibility. Controlling speed limits on highways, for instance, is designed to protect individuals from danger to self or others. Control only becomes evil when it is used for selfish or demonic purposes. Believers must learn to differentiate between the things they are to control and the things they are not to control. Patti Amsden discusses this in her book *The Law of Boundaries*:

The concept of boundaries presents both inclusion and exclusion. My home and property are domains which include me, my family, and any to whom I extend an invitation; but they exclude all persons who do not legally have admittance. Those who are excluded may not enter, use my property as their own, buy or sell my property, or in any wise usurp themselves as owners of that which is mine. Those who are included inside the boundary must steward the domain, because boundaries define who owns and who manages. The owner of the property is legally responsible for what happens on his or her property. Non-owners are not responsible for the property. A boundary mandates that I identify that which I own and that which is owned by another. Taking responsibility for my portion is required; taking ownership of another's is trespassing his boundary.[1]

We are responsible for our own will—our property. Even God does not trespass our will. He gives us the right to choose. Satan, however, will control a person's will, if given the chance. He trespasses boundaries by trying to control people's wills and actions. Sometimes the enemy uses God's people and those close to us to do his work of control. Witchcraft is a form of control that deceives, intimidates and manipulates through sorcery; and it is a seductive, guileful influence.

IDENTIFYING A CONTROLLING SPIRIT

A number of characteristics help identify a controlling spirit. One characteristic is that the controller attempts to prevent others from fulfilling their call. Controllers will try to convince us that we really don't have a call and therefore should not try to do something God has obviously not called us to do. Controllers attempt to convince us that we will be far more successful if we will help them fulfill *their* call, rather than pursuing our own. We must therefore realize and remember that the enemy does not want us to fulfill our God-given destiny. If he can talk us out of it, he will. To guard against being seduced by the enemy, we must listen to the Spirit of God and resist the doubts and insecurities the enemy sends our way. God never calls us to do what we are capable of doing on our own; He calls us to do the impossible. Then when the job gets done through His empowering grace, He gets all the glory!

Another characteristic of controlling spirits is that we are threatened if we do not do what the controller wants. Fear is not of the Lord, and the controller tries to use fear to control others. Some of the religious leaders of the first century attempted to threaten the apostles.

But in order that it may not spread further among the people and the nation, let us warn and forbid them with a stern threat to speak any more to anyone in this name [or about this Person] (Acts 4:17, *AMP*).

Peter and John refused to submit to the threatening words that tried to control them.

But Peter and John replied to them, Whether it is right in the sight of God to listen to you and obey you rather than God, you must decide (judge). But we [ourselves] cannot help telling what we have seen and heard. Then when [the rulers and council members] had further threatened them, they let them go, not seeing how they could secure a conviction against them because of the people; for everybody was praising and glorifying God for what had occurred (Acts 4:19-21, *AMP*).

Controlling people can be exceptionally religious and may even use Scripture to threaten others. Scriptures, such as the one that follows, can be used as a hammer to cause people to overlook the abuse they are receiving.

Do not touch My anointed ones, and do My prophets no harm (1 Chron. 16:22).

When we begin to resist the control, the above Scripture is sometimes used to convince us that we are judging a servant of the Lord. But when we are spiritual, we are to judge all things (see 1 Cor. 2:15), such as prophetic words, doctrine and the fruit of a person's life—good or bad—including a controlling spirit.

Controlled people feel trapped in their situations and unable to find hope of ever being free. Often we see this pattern in the lives of those who have been abused. Controllers cause their victims to feel ignorant and immature. Those who are being controlled then become persuaded that they need the controller. After a time of believing this, they then become convinced that they are not smart enough to make it without the controller. Controlled people feel ignorant and incapable of making right decisions. All of this, of course, is the goal of controllers, who want others to be dependent upon them. The truth is that *the controller needs the other person to feed his or her need to be needed.*

I remember battling for years to try to maintain a close relationship with a loved one; however, a spirit of jealousy and envy was constantly rising up. Whenever I had lunch with a friend, the controller got jealous. I was reminded of how I had left out the controller and how hurtful it was. The person would then go on to say that ministry was received in spite of my behavior. Guilt is a form of control. If the person can make us feel guilty for our actions, we will be effectively controlled.

A controller does not want us to have other close relationships because those relationships threaten the person's control over us. It is important to resist the guilt and to realize the Lord puts various people in our lives to keep us balanced and emotionally healthy.

Controllers use several methods to cause others to do what they want. Often they will try to make people feel guilty for refusing to do their bidding. "After all I have done for you," they whine. "Now look at what you're doing to me." According to controllers, others owe them a debt that can never be paid. Any small kindness the controlling person has done for others in the past is then held over their head to keep them in bondage to the controller.

If guilt does not work, tears usually follow. "At the worst time in my life, look at what you are doing to me," the person sobs. At that point the controlled person often backs off from the previous decision to resist the control, reasoning that maybe the timing is wrong. However, people who allow themselves to be controlled soon discover that there is never a "right" time for the controlling spirit to liberate them. A determination must be made by those being controlled to break free, in spite of the guilt and tears.

When guilt and tears don't work, controllers may become angry. Anger is a tactic that often works for them. Controlled people are fearful of confrontation because of the anger. As a result, controllers continue to get their own way because no one wants to face the outbursts of anger and condemnation. Those who are being controlled must understand that there is a demonic spirit in operation, and then they must respond in an opposite spirit.

> A gentle answer turns away wrath, but a harsh word stirs up anger (Prov. 15:1).

If the enemy can get us to respond out of the same spirit that is operating through the controlling person, he has won the battle. As we respond out of the Spirit of the Lord in a gentle but firm way, we disarm the enemy's weapons.

A controlling spirit will also use prophecy and spiritual gifts to control. Visions, dreams and prophecies are sometimes given by controllers to get others to do what they want. Controllers often come across as so superspiritual that others could never achieve their level. Controllers often warn others that they are not doing the right thing or that they are in danger if they go against the controller's wishes or advice. They imply—or even proclaim openly—that God has "assigned" them to watch over others. These controllers then use these distorted spiritual gifts to give "guidance" to those they wish to control. The problem is, the gifts are not from the Lord, and the controllers are not acting on God's instruction or under His anointing. The controllers' own soulish nature and demonic spirits are being sent to control others.

RECOGNIZING A JEZEBEL SPIRIT

A woman named Jezebel embodies a controlling spirit found in the Bible (see 1 Kings 16—21; 2 Kings 9; Rev. 2:20). Whenever a person seeks to advance in the call of God, a Jezebel spirit more often than not will try to stop the calling. We see this in the life of David. He had been anointed as king over Israel. As David moved forward in his God, the enemy was stirred.

> When the Philistines heard that they had anointed David king over Israel, all the Philistines went up to seek out David; and

when David heard of it, he went down to the stronghold (2 Sam. 5:17).

David was accustomed to resistance. He had been resisted through the years by a controlling king named Saul. Saul wanted to keep David from advancing by keeping him in an old place. He did not want him to fulfill his call but rather to serve Saul's vision. Saul threatened David, using anger in an attempt to control him. Saul wanted David to serve him by playing music so that his mind was relieved of torment. He did not want David to come into a new place and fulfill his God-given call. Saul is a good example of how a controlling spirit operates (see 1 Sam. 18).

David, however, knew he had a destiny. He could not be a man-pleaser but must be a God-pleaser. He was not warring against flesh and blood but against a strong demonic spirit. That demonic spirit was a controlling spirit—a Jezebel spirit. Although in the Bible Jezebel is a woman, the spirit is neither male nor female. This spirit will operate through both men and women.

Jezebel was the wife of King Ahab. She was a rebellious, manipula-tive queen. Like Jezebel of the Old Testament, the Jezebel spirit is independent and intensely ambitious for preeminence and control. The Jezebel spirit is superspiritual. Jezebel is not against all prophets, only the *true* prophets. In 1 Kings 18 we read the story of the prophet Elijah and the prophets of Baal. The prophets of Baal were controlled by Jezebel. Today, Jezebel still has false prophets and uses prophecy to gain control.

The spirit of Jezebel refuses to walk in unity, wanting to have its own way and refusing to submit to anyone. Francis Frangipane acknowledges the independence of this spirit and discusses the mean-ing of Jezebel's name.

It is noteworthy that the name "Jezebel," literally translated, means "without cohabitation." This simply means she refuses "to live together" or "co-habit" with anyone. Jezebel will not dwell with anyone unless she can control and dominate the relationship. When she seems submissive or "servant-like," it is only for the sake of gaining some strategic advantage. From her heart, she yields to no one.[2]

The spirit of Jezebel is like a spiritual cancer. It is aggressive and wants to kill the new move of God. It will steal the affections of new believers, the weak, the disappointed, the naïve, the troubled and the gullible.

Jezebel is typically found in a position of leadership. If not in leadership, this spirit seeks to influence leadership. The Jezebel spirit is strong-willed, religious and generally extraordinarily gifted. Often it appears extremely loyal and willing to volunteer. As this spirit gets close to leadership, however, it becomes privy to personal information. Needing someone to talk to, leaders find themselves revealing the secrets of their hearts to this spirit. When the time is right, Jezebel will betray the leaders' confidences in order to destroy the leadership by using knowledge of their personal lives.

The spirit of Jezebel loves to warn leadership about other people, often sharing a dream or vision concerning these people. The motive is to cause destruction to them because the spirit hopes to get rid of those who may discern the deceptive, controlling work of the Jezebel spirit.

COMBATTING THE JEZEBEL SPIRIT

The goal of Jezebel is to attack the purpose of God to restore the true prophetic voice to the Church. Jezebel will go to any length to silence the voice of the prophets and bring to a halt the prophetic anointing in the Church. Jezebel is a controlling spirit that the Lord warned the Church at Thyatira to deal with.

But I have this against you, that you tolerate the woman Jezebel, who calls herself a prophetess, and she teaches and leads My bond-servants astray, so that they commit acts of immorality and eat things sacrificed to idols (Rev. 2:20).

The Jezebel spirit is powerful and difficult to combat. However, the first weapon in walking free of its control is to recognize its influence. Identifying the enemy is vital to victory in warfare. We must ask the Holy Spirit to reveal where we have tolerated this spirit to operate in our lives. Repentance for allowing the Jezebel spirit to influence us begins a path to freedom. The Word of God is important so that our minds are renewed and free from wrong religious thinking. Thoughts should be centered on the Lord's will for our lives and not the will of a controlling spirit.

> Finally, brethren, whatever is true, whatever is honorable, whatever is right, whatever is pure, whatever is lovely, whatever is of good repute, if there is any excellence and if anything worthy of praise, let your mind dwell on these things (Phil. 4:8).

Not only should we allow our minds to be renewed into right thinking, we must also develop a Jehu spirit (see 1 Kings 16; 19; 2 Kings 9–10). Jehu was a king of Israel. He was sent by a word through Elisha the prophet to fulfill God's promise. Jehu and his men drove their chariots furiously toward Jezreel. Jehu slew the two kings of Judah and Israel. He confronted Jezebel and had her thrown down to her death. We must receive a warring spirit of Jehu and confront Jezebel. Only a Jehu spirit can destroy the Jezebel spirit. We must not be as the church of Thyatira, mentioned in Revelation 2, and tolerate its evil, manipulative, controlling ways. I like the way Francis Frangipane describes the Jehu spirit.

> There was something in Jehu's spirit that we must possess today in our war against Jezebel. While we must be compassionate toward those captured by Jezebel, Jehu had no mercy, no hopes for reform, no compromise or sympathy whatsoever toward this demonic spirit! Jehu ". . . trampled her under foot" (2 Kings 9:33). While she lay bleeding and near death, he trampled her beneath the feet of his horse!
>
> So with us, we must have no tolerance whatsoever for this spirit! *There can be no peace, no relaxing under our "fig tree," until*

Jezebel is slain! We must stop living for comfort as long as her harlotries and witchcrafts are so many in our land! We must refuse to settle for a false peace based on compromise and fear, especially when the Spirit of God is calling for "War"![3]

Pray and ask the Lord to put within you the same determination that Jehu had for conquering the controlling spirit of Jezebel. You have a calling on your life. Jezebel and controlling spirits do not want you to fulfill your call. A new strength and faith must be in you as you are chosen by the Lord to overcome Jezebel. Let God arise in the spirit of Jehu, and let His enemies of Jezebel and control be defeated!

THE REAL STORY
Overcoming Jezebel and Controlling Spirits in My Life

Testimony by Doug Fortune
Trumpet Call Ministry, McPherson, Kansas

Jezebel has many faces. Sometimes she needs a shave; she is not gender specific.

Often young unseasoned prophets are disfellowshipped because of their immaturity, as I was once. Let me introduce you to leader Smith (not his real name). He took me in to help heal my wounds. Later, I realized his ministry stemmed from insecurity. He needed to be needed.

However, as I grew in the Lord, my questions and hearing of God's voice somehow became a threat to him. I was growing into something very different from his ministry. This didn't set well, as he wanted me conformed to his image. He had invested a lot in me. I was no longer under his control, so in his eyes I was "out of control." I was labeled rebellious.

I had to respect his functional authority, while not coming under the control and condemnation, as guilt was his primary tool. I was not struggling with flesh and blood. My battle was fought on my knees as the Father showed me areas where I was harboring the same controlling spirit. Through repentance, I gained a compassion for leader Smith, as he was really a spiritual captive who needed to be set free. Keeping this perspective was the key to victory in this all-too-familiar scenario.

DISCUSSION QUESTIONS

1. Discuss some of the reasons why a person becomes a controller.
2. Is all control wrong? Why or why not?
3. When does control become wrong?
4. Control is a form of _____.
5. Describe some of the characteristics of a controlling spirit.
6. What are some methods used by a controller to achieve his or her goal?
7. Describe the Jezebel spirit.
8. What are some of the ways Jezebel influences leaders?
9. What is the first thing we must do to be free of Jezebel's control in our lives?
10. Who was Jehu? What did he possess that empowered him to conquer Jezebel?

Notes
1. Patti Amsden, *The Law of Boundaries* (Kirkwood, MO: Impact Christian Books, Inc., 1999), pp. 18-19.
2. Francis Frangipane, *The Jezebel Spirit* (Cedar Rapids, IA: Advancing Church Ministries, 1991), p. 2.
3. Ibid, pp. 12-13.

SECTION III

The Faithful

*His master said to him, "Well done, good and
faithful slave; you were faithful with a few things,
I will put you in charge of many things, enter into the
joy of your master."*

MATTHEW 25:21

CHAPTER 11

BREAKING OUT OF THE OLD PLACE

Heights always terrified me. I would never walk into elevators with glass enclosures. I remembered going to camp as a child and watching other children climb the steps of a forest tower. I was able to get only to the third step before carefully backing myself down to the ground.

Now I was an adult with three small children. The same fear of heights I experienced while climbing the steps of the forest tower at camp overwhelmed me as we drove around the rim of the mountains of Mexico. We were driving a missionary family from Texas to Guadalajara, Mexico. The family had been given a trailer to carry their household goods. My husband was pulling the trailer behind our car. When the car reached a speed of 45 miles per hour, the car felt as if it were going to turn over. I later learned the trailer was not balanced. The combination of the instability of the car and the height of the mountains caused a fear to rise up in me that I didn't know still existed. As long as I stayed on level ground, I didn't have to deal with the fear of heights. Therefore, I made it a practice never to go to high places—at least, not until the trip to Mexico.

"If you think the drive was bad today, just wait until tomorrow," the missionary warned me. "The worst is still ahead."

I wondered how it could possibly be worse than today. Tears streamed down my face as I remembered the drive through the mountains over the last three days. Nausea had been a constant companion on this trip. It was impossible for me to look out of the window of the car. The road wound its way around steep mountains with no shoulders on the road for most of the trip. My knuckles were white from holding on to the car. Fear seemed to overwhelm me. How thankful

I was at 2:00 A.M. when we were able to stop at a motel in Zacatecas. However, I spent the night tossing and turning in dread of what was to come. How could I endure one more day of the fear, nausea and torment I was experiencing?

FACING OUR FEARS

Early the next morning we started our final day's journey through the mountains to Guadalajara. As we rode along, I opened my Bible and read from Psalm 91.

> He who dwells in the shelter of the Most High will abide in the shadow of the Almighty. I will say to the LORD, "My refuge and my fortress, My God, in whom I trust!" For it is He who delivers you from the snare of the trapper, and from the deadly pestilence. He will cover you with His pinions, and under His wings you may seek refuge; His faithfulness is a shield and bulwark (Ps. 91:1-4).

I closed the Bible, unable to read any further, as the tears streamed down my face. "Lord, I have done all I know to do. I have prayed, confessed your Word, worshiped, bound, loosed and anything else I have been taught to do. Nothing has worked. If You don't set me free of this fear, I don't know what I will do."

With a sense of relinquishment, I put my head against the back of the seat and closed my eyes. About 15 minutes later I felt something break off my left shoulder. Startled at the sensation, I sat up straight. I had never before experienced anything like that. After straightening myself upright, my eyes fell on the mountains across the horizon. How majestic they were! Waterfalls cascaded down the sides; tall trees painted the landscape. "Lord, how beautiful are these mountains. You created all this for us to enjoy," I exclaimed. Suddenly, I realized something was different. The fear was gone. The sensation that had brought torment to me 15 minutes earlier had been transformed into a thing of beauty. Jesus had set me free!

How little I understood what had happened to me in those mountains. This incident unlocked my destiny in life. Had the Lord not allowed me to get into a situation where the hidden fear surfaced, that fear would have continued to hinder me in fulfilling God's call. Today I minister in many remarkable places. Sometimes I find myself on the top of the mountains of the rainforests in Malaysia. Watching young people sing "There's gonna be a revival in our land," I thank the Lord for that time in Mexico. I am now able to go into a Muslim country and help equip a young generation of Christians for revival. Had the Lord not allowed me to get into a situation where I faced my fear and allowed Him to deliver me, I could not minister in the places He is now allowing me to go.

A few years ago I returned to Zacatecas with a team of ministers and stayed in the same room of the same hotel where I had been many years earlier. Realizing the goodness of the Lord to me, I took a taxi to the highest hill of Zacatecas. As an act of gratitude, my husband and I stood overlooking the city. "Zacatecas, come under the lordship of Jesus," we prophesied to the city. "You were created by the Lord to give honor to Him." How wonderful to experience the freedom of the Lord and be used by Him to do things I had been unable to do in the past. Jesus helped break me out of the old place, so I could fulfill the destiny of the Lord for my life. He will do the same for you.

STANDING STILL

As we move forward in God's purpose for our lives, it is sometimes difficult to break out of the old places. Hidden areas must be dealt with in our lives. These areas are enemies that keep us from the success the Lord has destined for us. When moving forward out of the old place and an old season, there are times when it seems we are not making any progress. Just before breakthrough, there can be a time of standing still. God causes us to stand still and face the enemies that have followed us. The time of standing still is not designed by the Lord to cause us misery but, rather, to set us free.

The Israelites experienced a time of standing still as they were breaking out of Egypt. The miracle of deliverance was witnessed as the death angel passed over their homes and spared their firstborn, while claiming the firstborn of the Egyptians. Due to the judgments of the Lord on Egypt, Pharoah allowed the Israelites to leave the country. Not only that, they received an abundance of riches and supplies for the journey. They had left the old place but were not yet in the new place; it was a time of transition.

As the Israelites approached the Red Sea, the Lord spoke to them.

> Now the LORD spoke to Moses, saying, "Tell the sons of Israel to turn back and camp before Pi-hahiroth, between Migdol and the sea; you shall camp in front of Baal-zephon, opposite it, by the sea" (Exod. 14:1-2).

Can you imagine the thoughts of the Israelites when they heard this? *Camp? We want to move forward. A promise is in front of us, and we are not there yet. Let's not stop here. We need to keep moving forward.*

Yet the Lord had issued a command to stop. The visible enemy was not stopping them; it was God. He knew there were hidden enemies in their hearts. If those enemies were not dealt with, the Israelites would have no power to stand against the giants in the land where God was taking them. The goodness of the Lord had stopped them.

The first place the Lord told them to camp was Pi-hahiroth, whose name means "place of liberty." It did not look like a place of liberty. The Red Sea was in front of them, and they had no boats or airplanes to cross it. On top of that, Pharaoh had changed his mind about letting the Israelites go free, and his chariots and horsemen were fast approaching from behind. The wilderness had them enclosed all around. The situation appeared impossible, with no way out. However, this was destined by God to be a place of liberty.

Often we are in similar situations. The circumstances around us seem to enclose us on every side, and there is no way of escape. Then the Lord causes us to stand still in those times, so He can bring us into liberty. We can be in bondage and not realize it. I was in bondage to fear but did not realize it until I was faced with the fear and no way to escape.

During this time, the word of the Lord was being tested in the Israelites. God makes prophetic promises, but the word gets tested before it becomes ours. The enemy came to test the word of the Lord in the Garden.

> Now the serpent was more crafty than any beast of the field which the LORD God had made. And he said to the woman, "Indeed, has God said, 'You shall not eat from any tree of the garden?'" (Gen. 3:1).

When the enemy comes to question the word of the Lord, he always asks the same question: "Has God said?" He comes to steal the word of the Lord or to discredit it.

If the enemy can get us to doubt the word of God or to renounce it, he can keep us from coming into the promise of the Lord. The enemy does not want us to inherit the promises of God. In times of standing still, doubts can surface. We may doubt we have heard the Lord. An accusation may come that the prophecy was false or that a false prophet had spoken the word. It is important in these times to hold on to the word we have received. The Israelites had heard the promise of God concerning the land He was giving them. Fulfillment of that promise seemed impossible at Pi-hahiroth. The enemy of doubt had to be dealt with, or they could never stand against the giants in the land of promise.

In times of standing still, we must realize that the promise of the Lord is being tested. If we will ask God to help us believe Him more than we believe the circumstances, He will give us the strategy we need to move forward.

> But Moses said to the people, "Do not fear! Stand by and see the salvation of the LORD which He will accomplish for you today; for the Egyptians whom you have seen today, you will never see them again forever" (Exod. 14:13).

OVERCOMING THE FEAR OF FREEDOM

The next place the Israelites faced was an area known as Migdol, whose name means "a tower or fortress." It is so easy to blame others in times of difficulty. We blame our situation on others without realizing that God is revealing a hidden area that must be left behind if we are to enter into the new place.

> Then they said to Moses, "Is it because there were no graves in Egypt that you have taken us away to die in the wilderness? Why have you dealt with us in this way, bringing us out of Egypt? Is this not the word that we spoke to you in Egypt, saying, 'Leave us alone that we may serve the Egyptians'? For it would have been better for us to serve the Egyptians than to die in the wilderness" (vv. 11-12).

The temptation is to want to return to an old place when God wants to move us into our destiny. Even though we may not have enjoyed some of the situations in the past, we tend to remember only the good things. The Israelites remembered the food, safe homes and provision, however meager, they had in Egypt. They tended to forget the slavery, hardness of hearts in their taskmasters and captivity of their lives. There was a desire for the comforts and the familiarity of the past. Now that these were behind them, they blamed the leader for bringing them out into a fearful, insecure place.

Freedom can be frightening. Often when prisoners are set free, they commit crimes so that they may return to prison. Adapting to freedom is not easy. In prison others take care of the basic needs of life—food, shelter and clothing, even though these are bare necessities. Adjustment to limitations is often easier than to experience unlimited freedom.

Captivity limited the Israelites. They were limited by their knowledge and experience. It was difficult to imagine being in a place they had never experienced.

- How would they know how to function in the new place? In the past the taskmasters always told them what to do.
- Who was going to instruct them now? Maybe it would be better to return to the old life than to press forward into a place they neither knew about nor had experienced.

- They reasoned that someone else was responsible for their present discomfort. In times of change we go to self-preservation, rather than pressing into the purposes of God.

At Migdol we learn that the Lord is our tower and fortress. When everything around us is unstable, He is our stability.

And He shall be the stability of your times (Isa. 33:6).

The word "stability" refers to faithfulness. God who has been faithful to us in the old place is the same God who will be faithful to us in the new. The same promise made to Joshua before he led Israel into the Promised Land is the promise He has for us as He leads us into His purpose for our lives.

No man will be able to stand before you all the days of your life. Just as I have been with Moses, I will be with you; I will not fail you or forsake you (Josh. 1:5).

God becomes our fortress and our high tower in times of difficulty .

Encountering a Place of Deliverance and Fulfillment

The final place the Israelites encountered before crossing the Red Sea was Baal-zephon. The meaning of "Baal-zephon" is "Lord of the North." North in the Scriptures represents judgment. At Baal-zephon, God was going to judge the enemies of Israel. This would be a place of deliverance from the enemies that had harassed them all of their lives. The Lord would not allow these enemies to follow Israel into the new place. In the same way, the Lord often brings us to a place where He can deliver us from the enemies that have followed us for many years. He desires to free us, so we can move into the new place He has destined for us. Jesus is the Lord who judges our enemies!

What then is happening at this place of standing still before possessing the promise of the Lord? First of all, God is getting rid of our small thinking. He has planned so much more for us than we can imagine. Our mind-set tends to lock us into a limited place. Although we may acknowledge with our voices that He wants to do big things in our lives, our hearts don't always agree. Unbelief keeps us operating within a limited sphere.

I once read a story about a dog that was tied to a post for a lengthy period of time. The owner wanted to train the dog to stay within a designated perimeter. Throughout the time the dog was chained, he would walk around and around the post where he was tied. After some months, the owner released the chain that held the dog tied. Rather than running free over the large expanse of land around him, the dog continued in the old path. For hours at a time he would walk around and around the old familiar post, deepening the ruts he had already made in the ground. He could have run a great distance with his new-found freedom, but instead he remained in a small, limited place. God wants to bring His people out of limited thinking and prove He has given them unlimited potential.

At the place of standing still, God is also causing us to focus on the vision He has given us. We are unable to fulfill His vision in the present place. If we are going to come into the vision He has given us, we must do whatever is necessary to move forward. Destiny is not usually convenient. If Ruth had remained in Moab, she would not have met Boaz, and she could never fulfill her destiny. God called this Moabite woman—a highly unlikely person—to birth the lineage of the Messiah. Ruth had a choice. She could remain in a familiar place, staying where she had friends and family, knew the culture and had provision; or she could choose to follow Naomi, without any promise of financial security or friends. If Ruth chose to go with Naomi, the Moabitess would have to learn the ways of a far-removed culture. Ruth made the decision to focus on the vision of following Naomi into an unknown place for an unknown future. We are the recipients of Ruth's obedience, as she focused on her God-given vision. Others will be blessed as we too allow the Lord to move us forward out of an old place and into the place of fulfillment.

Moving In to the New Place

The Church is going where it has never been before. We are going to need a new level of faith for the new place. While in Egypt, provision was made for the needs of the Israelites. After the release from captivity, no guarantee was made other than the promise of the Lord for the new place. A new level of faith was needed to believe the Lord for things they had never had to believe for in the past.

Each year I ask the Lord to let me see my faith level. Since faith should continually grow, I want to be sure my faith is ever increasing (see Rom. 10:17). I need a new level of faith for each new season in my life. The Israelites would need a greater level of faith throughout the wilderness than they needed while living in captivity. The Lord was preparing them for the days ahead.

What does it take to break out of an old place and into the new? The first thing that is required of us is to deal with our fears. Fear will keep us from our destiny. One of the ways I deal with fear is to look at God's track record. I remember singing a song many years ago about counting our blessings and naming them one by one so that we might see what God has already done. As I remember the blessings of God in the past, fear of the future is removed. I can be assured that the Lord has never let me down—and He never changes (see Heb. 13:8). People may have let me down. Life and circumstances may have let me down. God never has! Therefore, He is not going to start now. He is always faithful. Fear has no place in the presence of faith.

The next thing to do to break out of the old place is to kill the "holy cows." Dead activities and mind-sets need a good funeral service. Sometimes we try to continue with things the Lord has finished. There was new life in these routines at one time. However, we are not in that season today. God has moved forward, and so should we. Traditional religious spirits will try to keep us in an old place, but there is no need to try to give CPR (resuscitation) to something God has decreed dead. We must bury the dead cow and go forward into the new place the Lord has for us.

In breaking out of the old place and moving into the new, there must be a fresh drawing near to the Lord. Our relationship with Him must grow deeper and stronger for the new season. The New Testament believer is challenged to approach the Lord in a new and living way.

> Since therefore, brethren, we have confidence to enter the holy place by the blood of Jesus, by a new and living way which He inaugurated for us through the veil, that is, His flesh, . . . let us draw near with a sincere heart in full assurance of faith, having our hearts sprinkled clean from an evil conscience and our bodies washed with pure water (Heb. 10:19-20,22).

As we draw near to the Lord, we can embrace the change and face our future without fear. A new level of faith arises, and we are released into a new place to fulfill our destiny. A realization will come that the Lord has not caused us to stand still to make us miserable. He has held us still so that we can confront our fears and see Him destroy our enemies! As we are empowered to break out of the old place of captivity, we break into the new place of freedom.

THE REAL STORY
BREAKING OUT OF MY OLD PLACE

Testimony by Tricia Miller
President, Miller International Ministries, Tyler, Texas

As a young girl, fear and insecurity bound me. I learned early in school simply to take a zero when it came time to give a book report. I had the loudest mouth on the playground, yet in front of the class I literally could not speak.

I remember the day I received a prophetic word saying that the Lord had placed a teaching mantle upon me. I truly thought the givers of the prophetic word had completely missed God, yet I knew He was continuing to move me in that direction.

As God began to call me into the ministry, all the fears and insecurities rose to stop me. In spite of the fact that I had been through deliverance ministry for fear and insecurity, I still had to face my enemies and overcome them. Even though God had placed a call upon my life and released a prophetic word over me, I had to choose to stand before a crowd and press through and overcome.

In the midst of this, I have discovered that my life is not my own. I will overcome every enemy in order to be obedient to my Lord. I refuse ever to take another zero because of fear and insecurity.

DISCUSSION QUESTIONS

1. Have you ever experienced an overwhelming fear? What did you do?
2. Name some enemies that are trying to keep you from your destiny.
3. Why does the Lord stop us before we get into a new place?
4. What is the meaning of Pi-hahiroth?
5. What is the question the enemy uses to steal or discredit God's Word?
6. What is the meaning of "Migdol"?
7. Name some ways captivity limits us.
8. What is the meaning of "Baal-zephon"?
9. What are several things that happen when the Lord causes us to stand still?
10. What are some things necessary for breaking out of an old place?

CHAPTER 12

TRANSITION CHALLENGES

We had looked forward to our vacation for months. Spending a relaxing week with two couples who were close friends was something we had long anticipated. After a few days of sightseeing we decided to enjoy a quiet evening together. Pam had brought a video she was excited about, so after dinner, we all settled down to watch a movie that would deeply impact our lives.

For several hours we witnessed the life story of Mohandas K. Gandhi. He was called Mahatma, which means "great soul." Gandhi was instrumental in bringing a powerful transition to the nation of India. He had been educated in law in England and then traveled to South Africa. For 20 years he worked as a leader and a fighter for the rights of Indians and other minorities who were oppressed and discriminated against by the apartheid government of South Africa.

Gandhi then returned to India and received the respect of his countrymen. He was elected president of the All India Home Rule League. Prior to Gandhi's leadership, the people used violence to fight for freedom. Under his influence, there was a transition of the people's vision onto a nonviolent path to freedom. Gandhi's vision for change involved nonviolent civil disobedience.

The struggle to change the old way of obtaining freedom was slow and extremely painful. In spite of obstacles and hindrances, India gained home rule in 1947. Gandhi was able to influence the vision of masses of people due to the respect they held for him as a person. Because they respected him, they were able to respect and accept his vision for change.

TIMES OF CHANGE

John C. Maxwell talks about Gandhi in *The 21 Irrefutable Laws of Leadership*. I like what Maxwell says about one of the effective ways leaders are able to bring people into transition: "The leader finds the dream and then the people. The people find the leader and then the dream."[1]

Transition involves moving from where you are into the fulfillment of the dream in your heart. Merely having a dream is no guarantee the dream will become reality. Gandhi had to take steps in order to bring his dream to fruition. He had to pay a price. Challenges will come to all of us, and we must be willing to meet them if we want to see our dreams materialize. Transition involves a process of change to move us from where we are to where the Lord has destined us to be.

One of the marks of spiritual maturity is being able to discern when God is ready to bring change.

> There is an appointed time for everything. And there is a time
> for every event under heaven (Eccles. 3:1).

Jesus reprimanded many of the religious leaders of His day because they did not understand times of change (see Matt. 16:2-3). God has planned strategic times for our lives. We need to be sensitive to discern when an old season is over and a new season has started.

As we come forth from the times of testing and purifying, the Lord finds those who have been faithful in the last season. He chooses them in the furnace of affliction (see Isa. 48:10). These people have been faithful in small things; they are then promoted as faithful ones. They are prepared for responsibility over greater things. These people are dead to self but alive to God. As Third Day (Resurrection) People, they are transitioning from the wilderness to the Promised Land.

THIRD DAY PEOPLE

Third Day People are those who no longer focus on their own individual needs. They have assurance that the Lord is going to meet their needs. They focus on the kingdom of God being extended in the earth.

These are resurrected people, full of the life of the Spirit. Chuck Pierce describes these people in his book *The Future War of the Church*.

> The third day is a day of resurrection power! As the Church transitions from the "second day" to the "third day," we can expect to see not only revival but also Resurrection power that will overthrow the demonic forces that have kept us from seeing God's will done on Earth. The new wineskin to receive this power is now being formed by the Holy Spirit, even as He is preparing the wine to be poured in. God is transforming the Church, preparing us to receive revelation for future victory. The Church is arising and the Kingdom is coming.[2]

The prophet Hosea spoke of a Third Day People who have been through the pain of the past season. They have experienced the wounding, healing and purifying of the Lord. These people come forth in resurrection life on the Third Day.

> Come, let us return to the LORD. For He has torn us, but He will heal us; He has wounded us, but He will bandage us. He will revive us after two days; He will raise us up on the third day that we may live before Him. So let us know, let us press on to know the LORD. His going forth is as certain as the dawn; and He will come to us like the rain, like the spring rain watering the earth (Hos. 6:1-3).

The Lord has brought us to the Third Day.

> But do not let this one fact escape your notice, beloved, that with the Lord one day is as a thousand years, and a thousand years as one day (2 Pet. 3:8).

The Church was born 2,000 years—or two days—ago. As we entered a new millennium, we now stand as the Third Day Church. We are transitioning into the promise of the Lord for our lives.

Under the leadership of Moses, the Israelites traveled 40 years through the wilderness. Although they had received the promise of the Lord for a good land filled with everything they would need, that generation never received the fulfillment of their dream. The vision during the time of the wilderness was still an individual vision. *I need food. I want water. I feel like a grasshopper in comparison to the people of Jericho.* The focus of the vision was on self and self-preservation.

God raised up another generation under Joshua that had the maturity of a corporate vision for extending God's kingdom. When the new generation crossed over the Jordan, the vision of the people was no longer on the Lord meeting their individual needs; the vision was that together they would bring change to entire cities and territories. The transition God had willed for them had occurred.

THE CHALLENGES OF TRANSITION

Several challenges are inevitable for those who transition into a new place. One of the challenges is that there must be dissatisfaction with the present place. Those who are content where they are will not endure the difficulty of moving forward.

A baby bird is content in the softly padded nest. The mother bird knows the time when the little bird needs to learn to fly. She carefully removes the padding. The place that had been comfortable in the past is no longer comfortable. Twigs prick the sides of the tiny bird until it is no longer satisfied where it is. It begins to look for ways to get out of the present situation. Soon it spreads its little wings in an effort to get into a new place. It does not take long before the bird is doing what all healthy, mature birds do, what it was destined to do—fly! Had the baby bird not become dissatisfied with its condition in the nest, it would never have done what it was designed by God to do.

The Lord brings a holy dissatisfaction in our present surroundings, so we will do whatever is necessary to transition into a new place. We then are able to do what we have never done before: We come into our full destiny in the Lord.

Another challenge we face with transition is excuses for refusing to change. I have observed many churches over the past number of years who failed to transition into a new move of the Spirit. One of the excuses I have heard from leaders is that they want to guard the reputation of the organization they represent. A need for approval exists in the lives of these individuals. Often they do not deny that God really is doing something new; however, they seek the approval of man above the approval of God. The Scriptures warn about seeking man's approval above God's.

The fear of man brings a snare, but he who trusts in the LORD will be exalted (Prov. 29:25).

Other challenges of transition include fear of losing control, failure and inadequacy. Third Day People are risk takers who are willing to go where they have never been before, freely receiving from the Lord new ideas and ways of doing things. They possess prophetic eyes to see where the Lord is taking them and have prophetic ears to hear what the Spirit of the Lord is saying to His people (see Rev. 2—3).

Even though people hear the Lord and know what He desires, people who embrace transition will face conflict. Some will not understand where the Lord is taking them. Misunderstandings occur when we are no longer able to do what we have done in the past.

Accusations will also come: "He thinks he is too good for us now." Although your heart has not changed toward people, your activity must change if you are going to follow the Lord. You cannot allow misunderstanding of the motives of your heart to hinder you in God's purposes for your life. As Jesus moved toward His destiny, He was falsely accused. After all, many people still viewed Him only as a carpenter's son. They could not accept the fact that He had a mandate from the Father to fulfill. How could He be a prophet? How could He be the Messiah? He was just the kid down the street, from the home of Mary and Joseph.

And they blindfolded Him and were asking Him, saying, "Prophesy, who is the one who hit You?" And they were saying many other things against Him, blaspheming (Luke 22:64-65).

Another challenge of transition involves the new connections God has for us in the new season. Recognizing the relationships the Lord has purposed for our lives will help us know with whom we are to connect. Some people can be snares to hinder us from fulfilling God's purpose (see Josh. 23:12-13). These people like to be around us because of who we are. They enjoy the blessings of God that come through us. We have a way of causing them to feel important and included in what we are doing. However, *they do not want to go where we are going.* They are not willing to pay the price to move forward in God's purposes. These people are time-consuming and simply enjoy the attention they receive from us. We must recognize the snares when they come our way. We can be kind and gracious without forming close connections that will hinder us from transitioning into the new place the Lord has for us.

Another connection to avoid is people who become leeches in our lives. These people never give anything to the relationship. They are always in need and always in crisis. The gospel works! It does not work for only a select few. It works for anyone willing to walk in the ways of the Lord. A new Christian needs time for transformation to occur in ways of acting and living. However, a person who has known the Lord for 10 years should have reached a place of maturity where the life of Christ is manifest. They should no longer be high-maintenance individuals. Leeches never seem to make progress. They are time and energy absorbing.

I remember a leech relationship in my life many years ago. Sarah was a Christian who had known the Lord for over 20 years. She could quote entire portions of the Bible, yet she never allowed the Word of God to bring transformation into her life. Sarah had a continual history of crises—some real, some imagined or contrived. These crises usually occurred in the evening when my family had just sat down together for dinner or in the middle of the night.

One morning at 3:00 A.M. my phone rang. It was Sarah's son, calling to let me know that his mother needed me to come to the hospital immediately. An intravenous tube was going to be inserted to give her a medication to prevent her blood from clotting. Knowing Sarah's medical history, I realized this was not a new procedure for her. It was, in fact, a minor procedure, and it was not life threatening. Sarah's son was a young adult and was planning to drive her to the hospital.

As I listened for the Lord to tell me what to do, He spoke a powerful word to my spirit: "If you continue to take Sarah out of the tight places, you will cause her to be a spiritual cripple. You will make her into a worm, rather than the butterfly I intend her to be." Wow! I had never before seen it that way. I thought I was only helping someone with a genuine need. God saw the situation through different eyes. He knew I was ministering out of human love, rather than His love. God's love is sometimes tough, but it sees beyond the present discomfort of the flesh to the true need in the individual's life. I asked Sarah's son to let me speak with his mother.

"I cannot come," I told Sarah.

"But I need you to be there," she cried.

"Your son will be there. The doctors and nurses who are at the hospital are very competent people. They will be there. I cannot do what they will do for you. Not only that, Jesus will be with you. I am going to pray for you right now, but I cannot come to the hospital."

I did not hear from Sarah for about three years after I declined to do what she had asked of me. Years later I received a phone call from her. She apologized for her attitude for the past three years. She said she had been angry and hadn't wanted to talk to me. However, the Lord had dealt with her, reminding her of the many things I had done for her in the past. He revealed her dependence on me, rather than on Jesus.

Sarah was no longer a worm crawling in the dust of life as a beggar. She had become a butterfly. Sarah was now able to soar to new places in the Spirit with a freedom she had never known. Together we laughed and cried over the phone at the wisdom the Lord had given during the 3:00 A.M. crisis. Sarah never turned back to her old life as a leech. She continued to grow and soar in the Spirit until the time she went home to be with the Lord.

New Wineskins

God has a Third Day People who have transitioned from worms to butterflies. They are new wineskins, prepared for the wine the Lord is pouring out in these last days. Old wineskins are not able to accept the fresh move of God. Jesus challenged the followers of His day to become new wineskins.

> And no one puts new wine into old wineskins; otherwise the new wine will burst the skins, and it will be spilled out, and the skins will be ruined. But new wine must be put into fresh wineskins. And no one, after drinking old wine wishes for new; for he says, "The old is good enough" (Luke 5:37-39).

A new wineskin is one that embraces new ideas. Old ideas about ways of being involved with church, worship, finances and many other aspects of our lives must change if the wineskin is going to be able to handle the new wine. We cannot say "The old is good enough." The old was new in its day, but it has become old in the current season.

Changing ideas is difficult for many people. Even the business world recognizes the difficulty in getting people to accept change.

> Rare is the person who can hear a new idea and embrace it on the first bounce with full, unreserved passion. Most of us take to new ideas with all the enthusiasm of a cat being forced into a swimming pool on a November day. Denial, tentative toe-dipping and stubborn resistance are common reactions.
>
> "The human mind," observes physician Christine Northrup, "is an organ uniquely designed to create antibodies against new ideas."[3]

Several years ago I heard a minister telling about a time when he was speaking at a church. Before the beginning of the service, the minister was taken into an office. One of the men who accompanied him pointed out an unusual picture on the wall.

"What do you see?" the man asked.

After gazing at the picture for several minutes, the minister replied, "I don't see anything. It looks like a lot of paint strokes that have no meaning."

"Look again," the man encouraged.

"I still don't see anything that makes sense," the minister responded.

The visiting minister left the room to speak to the congregation for the scheduled service. About a year later, he was invited to speak at the same church. Quickly he agreed to return. "I wanted to see that picture again," he explained. "I wanted to know what was in the picture that I could not see before."

As soon as the minister arrived at the church, he headed for the office with the unusual picture. After studying the picture for a while, he got excited.

"I see it! I see it!" he exclaimed. "There is a nest in the picture. There are baby eagles in the nest. I can see it now."

It took time before he was able to see the images hidden in the picture. At first glance he was unable to recognize what he was able to see later on. We are the same way. When the Lord brings a new move of His Spirit, we cannot always see what He is doing in the beginning. We say "The old is good enough." However, if we will keep our minds open, the Lord will transition us into a new wineskin. The purpose of transition is transformation. The Lord desires to transform us so that we may help bring His transforming love to people, cities and nations. Third Day People are those who will embrace the challenges of transition and be used by the Lord as world changers.

THE REAL STORY
TRANSITION CHALLENGES IN MY LIFE

Testimony by Dr. Freda Lindsay
Cofounder and Chairman of the Board Emeritus
Christ For the Nations, Inc., Dallas, Texas

It was November 14, 1937, Gordon's and my wedding day in Portland, Oregon. The festivities over, we looked for a fourth-rate hotel—one we could afford for one night. After checking in, Gordon said, "Let's begin our married life by kneeling and rededicating our lives to God." Today, 64 years later, I share with you the results.

And though the Lord gives you the bread of adversity and the water of affliction . . . Your ears shall hear a word behind you, saying, "This is the way, walk in it" (Isa. 30:20-21, *NKJV*).

Trials and tests will surely come, but God has promised victory! The key to weathering those trials and making needed transitions is to first establish your manifesto. Ours was and is, Go into all the world and preach the gospel to every creature (see Mark 16:15).

Reflecting on our lives, we've been in many battles:

- I was dying of tuberculosis at age 24, but God healed me. Today at age 87, I'm still active in ministry.
- Several severe accidents have come to our family, as well as to some of our workers.
- We experienced fires, floods and disappointments in some ministers who fell through sin.
- Gordon's sudden heart attack and death in 1973 was a hard blow, and some expected the ministry to fold. But we had established our manifesto!

To date, Christ For the Nations has helped build over 10,800 native churches worldwide; 43 Bible schools overseas; a literature program supplying literally millions of Gordon's books in 78 languages, plus Bibles; a Dallas campus of 75 acres, with facilities for its 2,500 people, including a 1,200-student body receiving training as World Changers in English and Spanish, with about 250 internationals enrolled each year (the school has over 27,000 alumni from 100 nations); furnished food, clothing and 20- and 40-foot metal containers to disaster survivors.

Now we say, "Thank You, dear God, for choosing us to help spread Your glorious truth worldwide."

D ISCUSSION   Q UESTIONS

1. What is the focus of Third Day People?
2. Explain the Third Day and why it is significant to us today.
3. What was the vision of the Israelites under the leadership of Moses? What was the vision at the crossing of the Jordan under Joshua?
4. Why does the Lord bring dissatisfaction into our lives?
5. What are some challenges of transition?
6. Describe some of the possible negative relationships in our lives.
7. What can we do so that the Lord can make us into new wineskins?

Notes

1. John C. Maxwell, *The 21 Irrefutable Laws of Leadership* (Nashville, TN: Thomas Nelson, Inc., 1998), p. 145.
2. Chuck D. Pierce and Rebecca Wagner Sytsema, *The Future War of the Church* (Ventura, CA: Renew Books, 2001), p. 75.
3. "It's a Lousy Idea. I Hate It." *Business Review*, vol. 13, no. 12 (1998), p. 1.

CHAPTER 13

NEW LEVEL, NEW DEVIL

My husband, Dale, has always loved trains. As a matter of fact, we still have some of the Lionel and American Flyer trains he enjoyed as a child. We have taken rides on trains all over the world. He especially enjoys the ones with steam engines.

While vacationing in Washington State a few years ago, we heard about an old abandoned train tunnel. Dale could not wait to see it! After receiving directions from a local resident, we drove up the narrow dirt road and parked our car. Walking alongside the steep incline through thick bushes and briars was a real challenge. I kept thinking, *What's a nice girl like me doing in a place like this?* Nevertheless, my husband was determined to find the location of the old train accident that the railroad owners seemed to want to forget.

Steep mountains that reach new levels can be exciting to talk about or to view from a distance. However, the forerunners who reach those heights often tell stories of the difficulties and dangers in accomplishing such feats. Longtime residents of Stevens Pass continue to tell the story of the tragedy of a Great Northern Railway train caught in an avalanche. Many history books of that area fail to tell the whole story.

On March 1, 1910, the town of Wellington was buried by a massive snow slide that claimed 101 lives. Two passenger trains, three steam engines and all four electrics were buried. The damage was so extensive that it took work trains nine days to reach the site—which GN quickly renamed Tyre.[1]

Lives of train personnel were lost in the rescue attempt. Just before they completed the task, an avalanche came down the mountain and killed the workers and all the passengers on the train.

Shortly after the avalanche, the railroad company cut a new and safer path through the mountains. The accident was such a tragedy that those involved in the railroad industry scarcely mention that part of its history. There are no markers to commemorate the scene of the accident. People who want to see it must talk to local residents and then climb through the underbrush until they discover the forgotten tunnel and partial railway that remains.

PRESSING THROUGH
THE DIFFICULTIES

Which, of course, is exactly what we did. As Dale and I neared the old tunnel, I found myself dodging bees from every direction. Where did they come from? I noticed my arms and legs were scratched from briars, and the bees were swarming all around me. The road below where we parked had been much better than this. At least there were no swarming bees or prickly briars down there. I felt I would be blessed indeed if I got out of that place unharmed.

Suddenly, there it was—the old train tunnel. Abandoned, forgotten by most, today it stands as a part of history that helped forge a better way for future generations who would be able to safely navigate the high steeps of terrain because of the accident and loss of life that had taken place there. It seemed to be such an evil tragedy, and yet it would ultimately be used for mankind's good (see Gen. 50:20).

Most people would never press through the difficulties to discover this place that was so off the beaten track and out of the ordinary. Even though people could live a seemingly safe and secure life below the mountain, they would miss a lot. Avalanches, abandoned train tunnels, swarming bees and scratchy briars are certainly not my greatest enjoyment. In the midst of this, however, I somehow felt connected with destiny. I stood with a former generation of pioneers who were willing to help navigate through the high places to secure the destiny of future generations.

A new level in our walk with the Lord will bring us face-to-face with new enemies. As we climb to higher places in the Spirit, there will be new challenges and foes to conquer. I once heard someone say, "New level, new devil." Each advancement in the Lord brings with it new obstacles to overcome.

Young David in the Bible had to learn to defeat the lion and the bear before he was able to be victorious over Goliath. At a young age David had a shepherd's heart for those who symbolized the people of God. Throughout his life there are instances of David sacrificing his own safety and comfort for the sake of God's glory. A mature servant of the Lord is always seeking to bring glory to God. Personal sacrifice is not even a consideration. God's purposes and His glory being released in the earth propel the faithful ones through every obstacle. Faithfulness in the last season prepares us for greater exploits in the new season. David had been faithful among the sheep entrusted to his care as a youth. He defended them from the lion and the bear. It was faith in the living God that enabled him to perform such feats. Genuine faith is an infallible mark of God's chosen and faithful servants.

David was willing as a youth to fight the lion and bear in order that he might see God's glory released in the earth. Psalm 132:1-6 mentions the pastures of Ephrathah as a place where David developed the desire for a habitation for the Lord.

> "I will not give sleep to my eyes or slumber to my eyelids; until I find a place for the LORD, a dwelling place for the Mighty One of Jacob." Behold, we heard of it in Ephrathah; we found it in the field of Jaar (vv. 4-6).

HAVING A SHEPHERD'S HEART

The heart of a servant was evident in David from his early years. He desired God's glory in the earth, and he knew it would come as a result of the shepherd's heart that loved the sheep and would stand against the enemies of the Lord.

Later, after David had completed his service in the court of King Saul, the young shepherd returned to feed his father's sheep. The exalted position in the king's palace did not spoil him for humble service in the kingdom of God. I love what Arthur Pink says on this subject:

> Fellow-servant of God, your sphere may be an humble and inconspicuous one; the flock to which God has called you to minister may be a small one; but *faithfulness* to your trust is what is required of you. There may be an Eliab ready to taunt you, and speak contemptuously of "those few sheep in the wilderness" (1 Sam. 17:28), as there was for David to encounter, but regard not their sneers. It is written, "His lord hast been faithful over a few things, I will make thee ruler over many things; enter thou into the joy of thy Lord" (Matt. 25:21).[2]

After the Lord used David to release King Saul from a tormenting spirit, he returned to his father's sheepfold. Although he knew he was destined for kingship, he also knew the preparation for the exalted position would come not from natural training, nor would it come from degrees, theological creeds or the wisdom of man. Success and victory come as a result of living in the secret place of the Most High (see Ps. 91). Learning how to cast down imaginations and every high thing that exalts itself against the knowledge of God and to bring every thought captive to the obedience of Christ causes us to conquer the enemy in private. Later, we will enjoy victory when we meet the enemy in public.

In obedience to his father's command, David took food and returned to Saul's army to check on his brothers. How surprised he was when he arrived! Saul's well-trained army and its leaders stood in terror of an enemy named Goliath. Goliath is a symbol of the enemy that seeks to terrify and bring into captivity those who bear the name of the Lord. Goliath continued to mock the army of Israel twice a day for 40 days. The number 40 speaks of a time of testing. It was obvious that Saul and his army were not in communion with God. Their trust was in their natural abilities and natural weapons. David's trust was not in the natural realm but in the spiritual. His faith had been developed on the hillside among the sheep as he experienced God's help in killing the lion and the bear. Faith had grown within him. Now he was prepared for a new level of warfare. David had the assurance that the same God who had helped him in the past would give him victory in the present situation.

Although his brother Eliab misunderstood him, David was not deterred in his mission. Saul attempted to discourage David and offered him his armor. David knew victory could not be attained through carnal, natural resources. Even the enemy, Goliath, taunted him. Amazed that no one looked beyond the circumstance and perceived the root of the problem, David demanded an answer.

Is there not a cause? (1 Sam. 17:29, *KJV*).

David had a cause. His cause was the victory and glory of God. Why should an uncircumcised Philistine hold God's people in fear and defeat? God helped David triumph over the lion and bear in earlier years. Now at this new level, God would cause him to experience victory over this new devil, Goliath.

Releasing God's Power

A person walking by faith will be misunderstood and mocked in the day of battle, but faith must be tested. David revealed the secret of his confidence before the enemy. He spoke a prophetic proclamation and declaration of victory.

Then David said to the Philistine, "You come to me with a sword, a spear, and a javelin, but I come to you in the name of the LORD of hosts, the God of the armies of Israel, whom you have taunted. This day the LORD will deliver you up into my hands, and I will strike you down and remove your head from you. And I will give the dead bodies of the army of the Philistines this day to the birds of the sky and the wild beasts of the earth, that all the earth may know that there is a God in Israel, and that all this assembly may know that the LORD does not deliver by sword or by spear; for the battle is the LORD's and He will give you into our hands" (1 Sam. 17:45-47).

Faith now brought God onto the scene. David spoke words that released the power of God. Words are used by the Lord to create either victory or defeat in the day of battle. When God created the world, He used words to speak it into being (see Gen. 1). Even now that He has assigned us to be His representative in the earth, He still uses words to create. We are His voice in the earth.[3] Releasing faith-filled words into the atmosphere causes the will of the Lord to be established in the earth. God came alongside David as a result of his boldness to declare the victory of the Lord ahead of time in the face of the enemy.

The wicked flee when no one is pursuing, but the righteous are bold as a lion (Prov. 28:1).

In the midst of battle, God was preparing David for his destiny. Although he was in training through the lesser battles with the lion and the bear, David now encountered a greater battle with Goliath. However, Goliath was still part of David's training. The Lord was preparing David to rule and reign in greater levels of authority. He would later fulfill his God-given mandate to rule and reign over cities and territories. You and I have the same mandate (see Gen. 1:26-28; Matt. 28:18-20).

God has a people in the earth who understand they are destined to rule and reign with Christ Jesus. One of the ways they are equipped for this task is through intercession. These people release the word of the Lord to set in order things that are out of order. We sometimes refer to this as "governing intercession." Dutch Sheets, in his book *Intercessory Prayer*, gives a good portrayal of intercession and our role as representatives of Jesus in the earth.

Intercessory prayer is an extension of the ministry of Jesus through His Body, the Church, whereby we mediate between God and humanity for the purpose of reconciling the world to Him, or between Satan and humanity for the purposes of enforcing the victory of Calvary.

Christ needs a human on the earth to represent Himself through just as the Father did. The Father's human was Jesus; Jesus' humans are us, the Church. He said, "As the Father has sent Me, I also send you" (John 20:21).

The concept of being sent is important and embodies the truths of which we have been speaking. A representative is a "sent" one. Sent ones have authority, as long as they represent the sender. And the importance or emphasis is not on the sent one but the sender. The setting of conditions and the ability to carry out or enforce them is all the responsibility of the sender, not the sent one. For example, an ambassador representing one nation to another is a sent one. He has no authority of his own, but he is authorized to represent the authority of the nation sending him.[4]

LEARNING TO GOVERN

We must understand our role as sent ones, those who have authority to govern in our given areas of responsibility. Some of the definitions Webster gives for the word "govern" are

- to exercise authority over; rule, administer, direct, control, manage;
- to influence the action or conduct of; guide; sway;
- to hold in check; restrain; curb.[5]

Governing intercession is the ability to represent Jesus in exercising authority over the power of darkness. It is the authority to rule, to direct situations or to control, manage and administer the will of the Lord in the earth. Governing intercession influences the action, or conduct, of evil spirits and holds in check, or restrains, ungodly behavior that resists the Lord's will.

Governing intercession operates on three levels. The first level involves our own personal lives. We must learn to govern our own thoughts, actions and character before we can govern other situations.

God's principles are always the same. David's first anointing was among his own brothers (see 1 Sam. 16:13). As David was faithful in that arena, the Lord released the anointing as king over Judah (see 2 Sam. 2:4). Once again, David was faithful to the Lord and used the authority delegated to him for God's purposes. Finally, David reached a place where he received a third anointing. He was anointed king over all Israel (see 2 Sam. 5:3), as was prophesied many years before by the prophet Samuel (see 1 Sam. 16:13).

We must first learn to govern our own personal lives in private households and those close to us.

> He who is slow to anger is better than the mighty, and he who rules his spirit, than he who captures a city (Prov. 16:32).

Ruling our own spirit comes before ruling over powers of darkness.

In his book *Rebuilding the Real You*, Pastor Jack Hayford discusses the way Nehemiah required the people of Jerusalem to govern their individual lives. They could not rebuild a geographical city if their own lives were out of order.

> Nehemiah was *serious* about the subject of responsibility. He required the people to maintain their lives and their city under divine government. This text clearly teaches how the goal of any restoration program God has is to beget responsible self-government instead of slothful self-indulgence. The Holy Spirit wants the Jerusalem of your life to be a city of the great King—one where His Kingdom life is lived and served.[6]

In intercession we must take responsibility for our own lives. We speak the Word of the Lord to our emotions, thoughts and weaknesses. Rather than blaming someone else for our difficulties, we speak what God says about us. Learning to agree with the Word of the Lord releases us from the past and sets us on a new path of victory.

The apostle Paul learned to use the difficulties he encountered as a source of strength.

Therefore I am well content with weaknesses, with insults, with distresses, with persecutions, with difficulties, for Christ's sake; for when I am weak, then I am strong (2 Cor. 12:10).

Governing his own soul caused Paul to find contentment in whatever situation he faced. God wants the same from us. The Lord is going to have mature sons who mirror the image of the Lord in the earth.

For you have been called for this purpose, since Christ also suffered for you, leaving you an example for you to follow in His steps, who committed no sin, nor was any deceit found in His mouth; and while being reviled, He did not revile in return; while suffering, He uttered no threats, but kept entrusting Himself to Him who judges righteously (1 Pet. 2:21-23).

CHANGING NATURAL CLIMATES

The second area of governing intercession is in the natural realm. This area includes weather, storms, earthquakes, winds, floods and various other elements of nature. One of my first experiences with governing in the natural realm occurred during the early 1980s. I had just been installed as an area president of a large women's organization. The initial board meeting to make plans for the year was scheduled to take place on a Wednesday in Dallas, Texas. Tuesday night an ice storm hit Dallas and most of northeast Texas where the board members lived. I cancelled the meeting and scheduled it for the following Wednesday. Again, an ice storm hit the area on Tuesday night. Once more the board meeting was cancelled and rescheduled for the following Wednesday. In fact, the same thing occurred for six consecutive weeks.

When I listened to the news report during the sixth week and discovered a similar storm was forecast for the following day, I sensed faith rising up in my spirit. "You will not stop this meeting," I spoke to the storm. "I command you to stay out of this area." The next morning I awoke early for my trip to Dallas. The news report was warning drivers to use caution on the highways. Ice was forecast for the entire area.

I climbed in my car and headed west. Along the way I kept speaking to the ice storm and prohibiting it from sticking to the roadway. Large trucks coming from the Dallas area were covered in ice. I continued driving and binding the storm. "Ice storm, I bind you in the name of Jesus. You will not stick to the roads." Arriving in Dallas a couple hours later, I met an excited group of board members. "You must have been praying," they exclaimed. I told them how the Lord had caused my faith level to rise. I knew we had victory over the storm that had been preventing us from performing the Lord's will.

Later, while driving home, I listened to the radio weather broadcast. "We cannot explain what happened," the reporter commented. "For some reason the ice storm stopped just west of Dallas-Fort Worth and did not come into our area." I, however, knew what had happened. The Lord had released governing intercession, not only through me, but also through other intercessors. Intercession had governed over the natural realm and changed the natural climate in our area.

Jesus rebuked storms. He commanded them to be still (see Mark 4:35-41). As His representatives in the earth, you and I can do the same thing when He gives us the release.

Changing Spiritual Climates

The third area of governing intercession is in the spiritual realm. Believers can release proclamations and declarations that change the spiritual climate in an area. Dutch Sheets speaks of a time when he was ministering in England and was used in this type of intercession. The Lord spoke to Dutch and told him he was not there just to preach to the people in attendance; he was there to preach to the nation. Dutch was to declare the word of the Lord and call the nation back to righteousness, holiness, repentance and the Lord. He was to call forth the Lord's anointing, His fire and His presence into the land. Dutch approached those sponsoring the event and shared with them his instructions from the Lord.

Not wanting my hosts to think me too strange, I informed them as to what I intended to do. Then I did it!

I preached to the air.

I preached to the government.

I preached to the sinners of England.

I preached to the entire Body of Christ of England....
We received a call from England the week following our ministry. The message was, "Revival has broken out in London." Renewal had, indeed, hit the nation, with many people coming to Christ and thousands receiving a renewing touch of the Holy Spirit.

I would never presume that revival came solely because of our ministry. The years of intercession by many and the countless hours of selfless labor by hundreds of godly men and women had much more to do with it than anything our team ever could have done. What part did we play? Prophetic worship—declaring through pageantry and song the splendor, greatness, rule and authority of God, and prophetic declaration—proclaiming the will and Word of the Lord into the spirit realm.[7]

Today, we are hearing a new term used to describe intercessors who are sent to other nations and territories to proclaim, declare and intercede for the will of the Lord to be released in that area. Intercessory missionaries are being used in a way similar to that of how our national military uses air troops in times of war. The air troops go into an area to clear the way for the ground troops. Ground troops can then come in and take control over the territory. Intercessory missionaries are like air troops. They release the word of the Lord into the atmosphere. Evangelists, pastors and others can then see the lost come to the Lord, and they can establish churches and raise the Body of Christ to new levels of fruitfulness. The intercessory missionaries help change the spiritual climate of an area through governing intercession. They prepare the way for revival.

As we learn early in our walk with the Lord to operate in authority over the lions and bears, we are then prepared to face the Goliaths of cities, regions and territories. How exciting to be a faithful one who operates in the authority of the Lord and see His will come on Earth even as it is in heaven (see Matt. 6:10)!

THE REAL STORY
EAGLES OF GOD

Testimony by Apostle John P. Kelly
Ambassador Apostle, International Coalition of Apostles

On a chilly day I drove through Washington, D.C., to catch the red-eye flight to Guatemala City. I needed to arrive in time to represent the International Coalition of Apostles (ICA) from the United States for the formal commissioning of 18 of Guatemala's foremost apostles. This highly visible and historical event was important in both the natural and spiritual realms. I wanted to be prepared to address about 30,000 people. Only one obstacle stood in the way. I got there, but my luggage didn't! Now this might not pose a problem for the averaged-sized man, but I am taller than most in Guatemala. The suit they brought me was a short portly size. It was decision time: swallow my pride, get dressed and show up, or miss an important event in Church history. It was an easy decision.

At the city stadium, I was escorted to the room where the apostles were huddled, planning and praying. Denomination leaders and some missionaries had taken strong adversarial positions, claiming apostles are not for today. Some published their position in denominational periodicals and secular newspapers. Some gave rebukes and warnings over the radio and television. Then the Lord spoke to the apostles to "not attack back, but to go through the doors I have set before you. Keep on being and doing the work of apostles."

The event was a huge success. We were in full color on the front page of the newspaper, with me (in my poorly fitted suit) in the front row! Now the apostles are working and relating together stronger than ever. God pushed them through to a new level of authority. The Lord showed me some important lessons:

1. Ask the Lord for wisdom in every situation.
2. Be bold and courageous in your calling.
3. Build with like-minded people.
4. Don't focus on your adversaries; focus on the wide door for effective service God has prepared for you (see 1 Cor. 16:9).

DISCUSSION QUESTIONS

1. What is an infallible mark of God's chosen and faithful servants?
2. Why was David willing to fight the lion and the bear?
3. David had the heart of a _____.
4. Where must we live so that we can experience success and victory?
5. Whom does Goliath represent?
6. Where did David develop his faith? How did this help him when he encountered Goliath?
7. What was David's cause?
8. What happens when faith-filled words are released into the atmosphere?
9. What is "governing intercession"?
10. Name the three levels of governing intercession.
11. How can you gain the victory over the new devil you are facing at your new level?

Notes

1. T. O. Repp, *Railfan and Railroad: Stevens Pass—100 Years of Challenge* (Newton, NJ: Carstens Publications, Inc., 1993), p. 60.
2. Arthur W. Pink, *The Life of David* (Grand Rapids, MI: Baker Book House, 1981), pp. 11-12.
3. For a full discussion of this topic, please see chapter 5 in my book *Prophetic Intercession* (Ventura, CA: Renew Books, 1999).
4. Dutch Sheets, *Intercessory Prayer* (Ventura, CA: Regal Books, 1996), p. 42.

5. *Webster's New World College Dictionary,* 4th ed., s.v. "govern."
6. Jack W. Hayford, *Rebuilding the Real You* (Ventura, CA: Regal Books, 1986), p. 213.
7. Sheets, *Intercessory Prayer,* pp. 217-218.

CHAPTER 14

MENTORING THE NEXT GENERATION

Recently I watched a movie that was based on a true-life story. *October Sky* involved four boys in a high school in West Virginia during the late 1950s. A coal mine run by the father of one of the boys was the main industry in town. For generations, those living in this small town had worked at the coal mine, and it was considered their lot in life to work at this place, without any hope of doing anything different.

Then a young teacher came to the town and taught in the local high school. She challenged the students to reach for higher goals in life. She expressed her belief that they were capable of great feats beyond what previous generations had experienced. She challenged them to dare to dream big.

All this was done against the backdrop of a town caught in the grip of dysfunctional families, poverty and illiteracy. Regardless of their hopeless circumstances, however, four boys dared to accept as true what this teacher told them: They could rise to greater heights. They could break out of the vice that held them captive to less than their potential.

Under the mentoring of the teacher and a few others in the community, these four boys achieved great and noble positions in life, and they did it in the absence of encouragement from most of their families and friends. Each of the four young men eventually graduated from college and broke the barrier that had held generations in bondage. One of the young men became a rocket scientist for NASA and even trained astronauts. These men were able to go farther in their generation than the previous generation, because someone was willing to invest in their lives.

DYSFUNCTIONAL RELATIONSHIPS

Apprenticeship and mentoring are often-neglected aspects of both family and church life in today's culture. Many families today are dysfunctional, both in structure and relationships. We live in a disposable society. Products are used for our convenience and then thrown away. Too often we do the same in our relationships. If the relationship is no longer convenient or interferes with our own selfish desires, we simply discard it and seek a replacement. Divorce and separation in families is at an all-time high, even in Christian homes. George Barna gives some alarming facts concerning families in his book *The Second Coming of the Church*:

- One out of every four marriages has ended in a divorce.
- Two out of three adults say that a successful marriage is one in which both partners have total freedom to do as they choose.
- One-third of all married adults believe that adultery is an acceptable behavior.
- Cohabitation has risen by more than 500 percent in the past two decades (even though people who cohabitate prior to marriage have an 82 percent greater chance of divorce than do couples who marry without having first lived together).
- One out of every three children born this year will be born to an unwed mother.[1]

Not only do structurally and emotionally dysfunctional families affect the next generation, but so do the lifestyles of our current society. The demands of careers and high-paced living prevent the needed involvement of parents with their children. Family decisions are often dictated by the parents' careers, rather than by the relational needs of the family. Kingsley Fletcher talks about this in his book *The Power of Covenant*:

We have allowed our jobs to take first place in our lives, and our jobs—rather than God—determine where we live. We all have to feed, clothe and house our families, but if God is God (and He is), then He is well able to supply us with a job in the city or region where He has "planted" us. It is simply a matter of faith-activated obedience. When we allow our jobs to dictate such crucial family decisions as where we live, fellowship and raise our children, we are allowing our decisions to be wrongly dictated by the "god of the job."[2]

SACRIFICES MADE FOR RIGHT PRIORITIES

When our youngest son, Mark, was in high school, we encountered a very difficult financial situation in our family. The area in which we were living experienced an economic recession. Many people moved away in search of jobs. Knowing it would be difficult for Mark to leave his school and friends for the last two years of high school, we made the decision to cut budgets and trust the Lord for the finances for our family. At that time, our two older children were already attending college. Jobs were very scarce throughout the area, and yet my husband was selected out of over 200 applicants for a job that required only a 45-minute drive each way. His salary, however, was reduced to that of a new college graduate, even though he had over 25 years of experience. And yet, in our hearts, we knew we served a covenant-keeping God, who would be faithful to see us through.

During Mark's senior year, while he was enrolled in the early admission program at the local junior college, Dale accepted a position for a company in Dallas. We were able to sell our home and move one week after Mark finished his summer semester at the junior college. God was faithful to meet our needs during that time, and to place Mark's relational needs above the desire for financial gain in our own lives. We have never regretted the decision. The Lord has more than made up for any financial losses during that time. Mark went on to graduate from a four-year college and today is imparting spiritual core values into the life of his little daughter.

The core values once imparted by parents to the next generation have too often been relegated to educational institutions, media and peer groups. George Barna emphasizes the responsibility of parents to mentor the next generation.

> Together, husbands and wives must serve as the spiritual mentors of their children. For too long we have sloughed off the responsibilities of spiritually nurturing our children to anyone or any group that would take on that duty: Sunday schools, vacation Bible schools, midweek youth programs like Awana, Pioneer clubs, Young Life or Youth for Christ, or even media-driven influences such as Christian television or Christian videos. We have relied almost exclusively upon the efforts of others to train our children to be lovers of God.
>
> At the same time, these organizations were never intended to provide the primary spiritual influence and education of our children. By abandoning their responsibility to guide their children in spiritual matters, parents across the nation have seriously stunted their children's spiritual growth.[3]

LACK OF MENTORING

Not only do we see the lack of mentoring in our homes, but we also see it in the Church. Often we refer to the local church as "Pastor Bob's church," or whoever is the local pastor. The growth and success of the church body then centers on a single ministry gift. Highly gifted men often develop megachurches. However, when the gifted pastor is no longer at the helm, the church body usually diminishes exponentially. The focus has too often been on building man's kingdom, rather than building the kingdom of God. Why does this happen? One of the reasons is that there has not been a mentoring of the next generation.

We have focused on church growth programs, building projects, mission projects, budgets and various other programs. None of these programs are bad in themselves. However, the fruit of these projects is short-lived if there is not a younger generation to continue in the results of the efforts of the present generation.

Another reason there has not been a proactive emphasis concerning mentoring the next generation is that the Church has had an "escape" mentality. A large segment of the Church has focused on getting out of this world. Hundreds of books have been written, movies have been made, endless sermons have been preached and untold thousands of tapes circulated about the Church leaving the earth. The focus has been on *leaving*, rather than *occupying*.

This short-term mentality is evident in the types of buildings that local congregations construct. Contrast the typical metal buildings in the United States with the old formidable cathedrals of Europe. We don't build our buildings as if we expect them to last for generations. They simply provide a gathering place for a few short years.

We are God's covenant people, and He planned for us to walk in covenant relationships with each other. One aspect of covenant life involves the mentoring of the next generation. God's covenant blessings are designed to flow down through the generations. As His family mentors the following generations, those descendants will go farther and do more for the advancing of God's kingdom than previous generations.

FAITHFULNESS TO FUTURE GENERATIONS

In the Bible David understood this principle. He walked in a covenant relationship with Jonathan. After Jonathan's death, David did not forget his covenant responsibilities. He realized that not only did he have a responsibility to be faithful to Jonathan, but he must also be responsible to Jonathan's descendants.

David heard about Jonathan's son, Mephibosheth, and the accident that had damaged his feet. He asked that Mephibosheth be brought to live in the king's palace for the rest of his life. He would even eat at David's table. David restored not only all the land owned by Mephibosheth's father, Jonathan but also the land owned by his grandfather Saul. David assigned servants to farm the land for Mephibosheth, in order to provide an income and an inheritance for Mephibosheth's sons. In other words, David cared for his covenant friend's son in the same way he would care for his own sons. He understood the value of investing in the next generation (see 2 Sam. 9).

Another person in the Bible who helped mentor the next generation was the prophet Samuel. Samuel was a transitional prophet. He stood between an old move of God and a new move—the existing king, Saul, and the future king, David. Under the old religious system, King Saul was only interested in building his own kingdom. Not only did he fail to mentor his son, Jonathan, or the prophesied next king, David, but he also clung to his own exalted position. Out of envy, jealousy and insecurity, Saul persecuted David and sought to kill him (see 1 Sam. 16—2 Sam. 4).

How sad that there are ministries today operating out of the same flawed character as Saul's. Rather than seeking God's best for the younger, gifted generation, many oppose their anointings and God-given potential. Samuel was different. Up until his time, we see only individual prophets operating out of their own anointings. Samuel chose to mentor the next generation by raising up schools of prophets. He drew out of them the potential God had put within. Samuel understood the necessity of multiplying his ministry through many young prophets of the next generation. He realized his greatest conquest would be leaving behind a generation that would reach more people for the Lord's purpose than he alone could reach.

I love the story of Susanna Wesley. Although she had 19 children, she arranged to regularly spend time with each individual child. Many years later, we are still benefiting from the effects of her faithful mentoring. The Church would not be where it is today if the Wesley brothers had not made such an impact through encouraging methodical Bible study and their writing of many beautiful hymns of worship. Susanna's mentoring rewrote history for future generations.

Elijah is another example of mentoring. He found a young man by the name of Elisha, who was the son of a wealthy farmer. Elijah saw potential in the young man. He was willing to allow the inconvenience of investing in this future prophet to rise above his personal need for comfort.

Elisha understood the principle of impartation. He realized that his association with the older prophet positioned him for a greater portion of anointing. One day the prophet Elijah asked the young man what he wanted from him. Elisha did not hesitate to answer.

> Now it came about when they had crossed over, that Elijah said to Elisha, "Ask what I shall do for you before I am taken from you." And Elisha said, "Please, let a double portion of your spirit be upon me" (2 Kings 2:9).

Elisha was asking for the portion of the firstborn. During this era, the firstborn son received twice as much of his father's inheritance as the younger sons. Elisha viewed Elijah as a father and was willing to receive from him wisdom and mentoring. As a result of the impartation, Elisha performed twice as many miracles in his lifetime as his spiritual father, Elijah.

Many other examples of mentoring can be found throughout the Bible. Joseph mentored Jesus in the carpenter shop (see Mark 6:3). Paul instructed his own spiritual son, Timothy, to mentor the next generation and to raise up other faithful ones.

> The things which you have heard from me in the presence of many witnesses, these entrust to faithful men, who will be able to teach others also (2 Tim. 2:2).

PRINCIPLES OF MENTORING

What are some of the principles involved in mentoring the next generation? First, we must allow the Lord to make the connections in relationships outside our natural family. Often, an eager young person sees something they want in an older person. They may assume that the other person has the same desire. Often hurts occur through presuming a relationship to be more than the Lord intends.

Jesus had a certain level of intimate relationship with the 70 He sent out, a different level of relationship with the 12 apostles and a much more intimate level of relationship with the "inner three"—Peter, James and John. Finally, there was a special level of relationship with John, the youngest of the disciples, who was close to Jesus' bosom. Trust the Lord to give you the level of relationship He wants you to have with others. Often He wants young people to receive from more than one person, so they will be balanced in their walk with the Lord.

The next principle to keep in mind while mentoring is to be sensitive to each other's time. It is not necessary to have daily contact with a person in order for mentoring to occur. Often I have people tell me that I have been their mentor for years. In many instances, I don't remember ever having seen the person before; yet he or she may have been in my meetings, read my books or listened to some of my teaching tapes. These people were able to receive from my life without my awareness. Time together is precious but not always possible. Allow the Lord to provide those times together when both people can enjoy the relationship.

Another principle in mentoring is to be vulnerable. It is important for the next generation to know the defeats as well as the victories in life. I am part of a network of ministers and churches. We believe in investing in the next generation. At various times during the year we hold "Timothy Training" for the younger generation. The most frequently asked question by the "young lions" is "How did you get to do what you are doing?" They are not asking theological questions. They don't want Greek and Hebrew definitions for words from the Bible. They are not asking about eschatology. These young people want to hear the stories of how mature men and women of God were able to walk through the difficulties of life and still love the Lord with their whole heart. They want to know about the failures. They want to know about how they maintain relationships when difficulties arise. They are not as interested in the dynamics of *ministry* as they are in the dynamics of the *minister*.

Often in sharing with these young people, we tell of times when someone loved us, even when we were unlovely. God's love is not conditional. He is looking for those who operate in the same unconditional agape love that He extends to us. Mentoring will involve times of being unlovely. Since we are not yet perfected, there will be times when we may not look quite like Jesus. Looking beyond someone's exterior and seeing the heart will help us through those unlovely moments. We must refuse rejection and offenses and allow the Lord to help us look past the person's outward behavior to the need for God's unconditional love.

Mentoring the next generation has its own set of problems. However, it is God's plan for the advancing of His kingdom. We are the beneficiaries of those who have gone before us and paid the price so that we could be where we are today. How much less can we do for those who come behind us? I love the words of the song that asks that those who come behind us will find us faithful. My heart cries out, *Yes, Lord. I want to be one of Your faithful ones.*

THE REAL STORY
MENTORING THE NEXT GENERATION

Testimony by Dr. Kelley Varner
Senior Pastor, Praise Tablernacle, Richlands, North Carolina

How refreshing to hear and see the wind of God blowing the Church back to a generational purpose as we colabor in the ongoing purposes of God!

There is a difference between mentoring and fathering. In mentoring, one speaks and the other listens. In fathering, both speak and both listen.

My 20-year-old son, Jonathan, is my armor bearer and my friend. He has traveled extensively with me throughout the East Coast of the United States and has made three trips with me to South Africa.

Generations are different. When it comes to the kinds of food we like to eat, clothes we like to wear and music we like to listen to, we are different. These differences are not prejudices; they are preferences. Jonathan's generation stretches me.

Although I have faithfully proclaimed the gospel of the Kingdom since 1969, I am ever learning. To live is to grow. To grow is to change.

And spiritual growth denotes change after change after change (see Ps. 84:7; Rom. 1:17; 2 Cor. 3:18).

School isn't out yet!

DISCUSSION QUESTIONS

1. Describe some of the problems we see today in dysfunctional families.
2. Who usually imparts core values to the younger generation? Who did the Lord intend for this job?
3. What has been the focus of Church life in the past?
4. What are some of the reasons we have failed to mentor the next generation?
5. Why did David have Mephibosheth brought to live with him?
6. What did Elisha ask of his mentor, Elijah? What did that mean?
7. Discuss several principles in mentoring.
8. Will you be a faithful one and help mentor the next generation? Why or why not?

Notes

1. George Barna, *The Second Coming of the Church* (Nashville, TN: Word Publishing, 1998), p. 66.
2. Kingsley Fletcher, *The Power of Covenant* (Ventura, CA: Regal Books, 2000), p. 145.
3. Barna, *The Second Coming of the Church*, p. 192.

CHAPTER 15

EAGLES OF GOD

While vacationing in the Canadian Rockies, we visited the Colombian Icefield and the Athabasca Glacier. As I viewed the history in the visitor's center, my eyes were drawn to a plaque that described a couple of the pioneers who explored the area. Wooley and Collie were men who dared to brave the severe weather and hazards of the icefield. Unlike the negative responses of other explorers of the area, these men saw something positive. Rather than seeing the difficulties of the terrain, they saw an incredible challenge ahead to discover that which had been hidden from previous generations. The plaque bearing their names has this inscription:

> Wooley and Collie—It fell to two other explorers, Herman Wooley and J. Norman Collie, to finally realize the magnitude of what lay before them. The year was 1898 when Collie gave this breathless description of the Columbia Icefield: "A new world was spread at our feet: to the west stretched a vast icefield probably never before seen by human eye, and surrounded by entirely unknown, unnamed and unclimbed peaks." The mountains were no longer fearful, now they had become a challenge to be conquered.

Wooley and Collie were men who were willing to climb to great heights to pave a way for others. They were willing to explore the unknown. They sacrificed the comforts of life and risked their own lives for future generations. They climbed great heights to see the previously unseen. As mighty men, they were like great "eagles" in history.

THE NEED FOR EAGLE LEADERS

Eagle leaders are needed in the Church today. God is calling for leaders who will take the Church to a higher position than it has previously experienced. True leaders have some of the uniqueness of eagles. Throughout the Bible we see references to eagles. God is described as one who cares for His children like an eagle.

> You yourselves have seen what I did to the Egyptians, and how I bore you on eagles' wings, and brought you to Myself (Exod. 19:4).

> Like an eagle that stirs up its nest, that hovers over its young, He spread His wings and caught them, He carried them on His pinions. The LORD alone guided him, and there was no foreign god with him (Deut. 32:11-12).

The Lord planned for His children to be like Him; therefore, you and I are to have the same characteristics and nature as God. As faithful ones who have been called and chosen by the Lord, we are to exhibit many of the distinctive traits of an eagle. As we become eagles of God, we will obtain new strength for the journey.

> Yet those who wait for the LORD will gain new strength; they will mount up with wings like eagles, they will run and not get tired, they will walk and not become weary (Isa. 40:31).

CHARACTERISTICS OF EAGLES

One of the characteristics of eagles is that they are swift (see 2 Sam. 1:23; Jer. 4:13). Eagles are not procrastinators. They are not waiting around for a more convenient season to obey the Lord. Eagles have an ability within that causes them to be able to do in a short time what others take many years to accomplish.

Eagles also have incredibly keen eyesight. Eaglets are hatched with their eyes open. This characteristic reminds us that when we come to the Lord, He opens our eyes to revelation. We can see for the first time what we could not see before.

I pray that the eyes of your heart may be enlightened, so that you will know what is the hope of His calling, what are the riches of the glory of His inheritance in the saints (Eph. 1:18).

Eagles have large eyes located on the sides of their heads. However, they can see straight ahead. Most birds have sharp sight, better than men and other animals, but eagles are said to have the keenest sight of all. Eagles can spot their prey while soaring thousands of feet in the air. As eagles of God, we are able to see at great distances. Kingsley Fletcher, in emphasizing the far-reaching effects of covenant, discusses the necessity for long-term vision.

Myopia is a common vision problem afflicting a large percentage of the human race. Better known as nearsightedness, this condition prevents the human eye from focusing on distant objects. If this condition is left uncorrected, the sufferer is limited to focusing solely on things that are nearby or close up. Everything beyond their limited scope of perception is blurry and indistinct.

Any generation, nation, local body or family that attempts to exist apart from covenant is almost certainly suffering from myopia of a different sort. It takes the form of generational nearsightedness that threatens to turn all of their focus and attention toward "the now," the present, while leaving the destiny of future generations blurry, fuzzy, indistinct and, therefore, virtually irrelevant.[1]

Nearsightedness cannot be found in eagles. Their exceptional eyesight allows them to see at great distances. Vision for the future is constantly before God's eagles. They never settle for maintaining the present. Sometimes the future seems more realistic to them than the present situation. They are goal setters who dream big dreams and reach remarkable heights in the midst of adversity.

Eagles have learned to mount up when storms approach. As the storm nears, lesser birds head for cover. The mighty eagle, however, spreads its wings and, with a great cry, mounts upon the powerful updrafts and soars to great heights. The eagle is a symbol of America and is the only bird that has the ability to fly above the storm. In spite of the winds, thunder and lightning, the eagle seems to know instinctively where there is safety in the midst of destruction. Eagles of God see beyond the storm. They know how to find rest in the arms of the Lord and allow Him to carry them above all harm (see Pss. 23; 91). I like how John and Paula Sanford describe an eagle of God:

> Storms are a joy to him, for on their mighty updrafts he soars to heights of glory. And he does it effortlessly, letting the wind carry him where lesser birds must beat with frantic wings just to stay aloft. Just so, the eagle Christian sees behind the storm the surging, moving power of the Holy Spirit of God, and rises on wings of faith to rest in God's carrying power far above harm and destruction. He does not have to pump up his faith and talk himself into ephemeral moods of fleeting courage. He abides, restfully trusting the current of God's love, moving not by striving but by the soaring currents of God. The Lord himself bears him up. Others, seeing, try to huff and puff to his heights, and cannot understand his restful, easy soaring, ascribing it to the eagle rather than the winds of God's love. But the eagle knows the currents and turns here and there to catch the rising flow of life.[2]

Eagles have a staggering level of endurance. Their long broad wings and tails look clumsy when they are on the ground. However, these wings are able to support them when they fly. Eagles can glide long distances by holding their wings out stiffly. The long feathers in their wings are strong and stiff. They are shaped so that the air flows smoothly over the surface of the wing. When eagles soar, the feathers spread out like fingers and bend at the tips because of the upward pressure of the air. Like the eagle, faithful believers allow the wind of the Holy Spirit to cause them to rise up and endure the difficulties of life. Eagles are able to withstand hardships that would destroy more frail birds. Like the apostle Paul, eagles of God are able to press through difficulties for the sake of God's glory (see Mark 13:13; 1 Cor. 13:7; 2 Tim. 2:3). Conversely, after years of hardship and toil, the eagles take the initiative to renew themselves.

THE RENEWING PROCESS

Who satisfies your years with good things, so that your youth is renewed like the eagle (Ps. 103:5).

Some believe this renewing process occurs every seven years or more. The eagles do not wait for someone else to renew them. They are willing to receive help from others. At the same time, they are alert to their own need, and position themselves for renewal.

The eagles recognize the necessity to cast off the old and put on the new for a fresh new season. Often an eagle's wings become heavy with oil and dirt. The bird then finds a hiding place in a cave or in heights away from enemies. This is a time to experience renewal. With his great beak, the eagle pulls out his wing feathers and extracts each claw. Finally, he smashes his brittle beak against a rock until it too is gone. Left defenseless, this unique bird waits patiently until the beak, claws and feathers have grown back. The eagle then emerges into its new creation, stronger than before.

Sensitivity to the Lord during times of revitalization is essential, so we can be renewed. Time alone with the Lord is never wasted. He desires to strip us of all things that try to cling to us but are not of His nature. Standing bare before Him, we are then clothed in His likeness. Grief, sorrow and heaviness are exchanged for the joy and strength of the Lord.

To grant those who mourn in Zion, giving them a garland instead of ashes, the oil of gladness instead of mourning, the mantle of praise instead of a spirit of fainting. So they will be called oaks of righteousness, the planting of the LORD, that He may be glorified (Isa. 61:3).

Clothed with new strength, eagle Christians recognize that the Lord brings His people into new seasons. They then receive fresh revelation from God. Old mind-sets are renewed. Old ways of doing things change.

> When I was a child, I used to speak as a child, think as a child, reason as a child; when I became a man, I did away with childish things (1 Cor. 13:11).

MATURE EAGLES

Mature eagle Christians are prepared to encourage and equip the younger ones. They are similar to natural eagles in that they train the young. The young eaglets are cared for and fed until they are able to leave the nest and find their own food. The parents will continue to feed the eaglets for several months after they leave the nest, since they cannot hunt well enough at first to feed themselves. We greatly need to have the same caring concern for mentoring young leaders in the ways of the Spirit (see Deut. 32:11). John Maxwell discusses this in *The 21 Irrefutable Laws of Leadership*:

> An environment where leadership is valued and taught becomes an asset to a leadership mentor. It not only attracts "eagles," but it also helps them learn to fly. An eagle environment is one where the leader casts a vision, offers incentives, encourages creativity, allows risks, and provides accountability. Do that long enough with young people, and you'll develop a leadership culture where eagles begin to flock.[3]

Eagles live in high places known as aeries. An aerie is a dwelling on a height—a cliff or mountaintop. Eagles do not live in the low places of the earth. From that high vantage place, eagles see the world from a higher perspective. The Lord has His mature eagles that have mounted up in new levels of faith. They have built their houses on the rock of Jesus and are not destroyed in the storms of life.

> Therefore everyone who hears these words of Mine, and acts upon them, may be compared to a wise man, who built his

house upon the rock. And the rain descended, and the floods came, and the winds blew, and burst against that house; and yet it did not fall, for it had been founded on the rock (Matt. 7:24-25).

Many people are sensing a great revival coming in the earth. Revival requires a new strength and endurance. God is preparing those who will lead the way in releasing and sustaining revival. The laying on of hands and impartation of gifts help equip believers for the task God has given them. A spiritual dynamic is released to help eaglets grow into mature eagles of God. I discuss this spiritual principle in my book *You Are Anointed*:

> The Bible clearly teaches that the anointing can be given to another person. Paul reminded his spiritual son Timothy not to neglect the spiritual gift he had received from Paul. "For this reason I remind you to kindle afresh the gift of God which is in you through the laying on of my hands" (2 Tim. 1:6). Some of the anointing on Paul was transferred to Timothy and to other believers. . . .
>
> The anointing is necessary spiritual equipment for fulfilling God's purpose in ministry. How sad it is to see those who have a heart for God and yet labor in their own strength. Usually they end up in discouragement and defeat. Without the anointing there is a limit to what they are able to accomplish. The Lord has made a way for believers to be fully equipped for the task He has given them.[4]

God's faithful ones are humble enough to receive from others and yet remain strong in their walk with the Lord. They are empowered by the Holy Spirit to be eagles of God, destined to release hope, strength and courage to a world in need of our wonderful Lord and Savior— Jesus!

Dare to fly above the circumstances of this world. Dare to live a life beyond the *ordinary* through the power of an *extraordinary* God. Become the mature eagle of God you were created to be!

THE REAL STORY
EAGLES OF GOD

Testimony by Dr. Bill Hamon
Founder/President/Bishop, Christian International Ministries
Santa Rosa Beach, Florida

It is very important for all saints to learn the principles for an over-coming life. Forty-eight years ago, I was ordained into full-time ministry at age 19. My wife and I are often asked how we have successfully maintained and progressed on our journey.

My life and ministry have been full of challenges and transitions, especially since we have pioneered in apostolic and prophetic ministry. There are several truths we learned that took us from being *called* to *chosen* and then on to *faithfully following through*. I call that process going from calling to commissioning. The biblical examples of Joseph, David and Jesus are my greatest inspiration and encouragement. It stabilized me to know that God is more interested in the messenger than the message and more interested in the man than his miraculous ministry.

The truth of Romans 8:28-29 kept me from becoming too discouraged during God's process of taking me from calling to commissioning. When we know and believe that all things work together for our good because we love God and are called according to His purpose, we are enabled to make it through anything.

The highest calling in God's kingdom is not being the greatest apostle or prophet, nor the pastor of thousands; rather, the highest calling is being conformed to the image of Jesus Christ. This knowledge kept me going when I seemed to fall. God is always at work doing a work either in us or through us. Whether we are going through a winter, spring, fall or summer season, we are still abiding in God's orchard.

I could give numerous experiences that I have gone through that have proven these truths are real, that enabled me to go from calling to commissioning. We all can progress from being called to chosen to faithfully fulfilling our calling and destiny in God.

DISCUSSION QUESTIONS

1. What is a characteristic of God that can be compared to an eagle?
2. Name several characteristics of eagles. How are eagles of God similar in their nature to eagles of the wild?
3. How does myopia cause people or nations to become irrelevant?
4. How does the eagle handle storms?
5. Describe the renewing process of the eagle.
6. What is an aerie? Where is it located?
7. What are two things that help empower believers for their God-given tasks?
8. Are you ready to become the eagle of God you are destined to be?

Notes

1. Kingsley Fletcher, *The Power of Covenant* (Ventura, CA: Regal Books, 2000), pp. 86-87.
2. John and Paula Sanford, *Restoring the Christian Family* (Tulsa, OK: Victory House, Inc., 1979), p. 311.
3. John C. Maxwell, *The 21 Irrefutable Laws of Leadership* (Nashville, TN: Thomas Nelson Publishers, 1998), p. 140.
4. Barbara Wentroble, *You Are Anointed* (Ventura, CA: Renew Books, 2001), pp. 162-163.